Obsidian Point
A Triptych

by
Ken McCullough

**Obsidian Point
A Triptych
by
Ken McCullough**

© 2003 by Ken McCullough
All rights reserved
Cover Painting © 2003 by Lisa Nankivil
Published by
Lone Oak Press
Red Wing, Minnesota
info@loneoak.org

ISBN 1-883477-62-X
Library of Congress Control Number: 2001090389

for

Galway

Orion

and Lynn

This book consists of three parts:
two long sequences of poems and an essay,
with some shorter pieces as "connective tissue."
All three parts are set on Mt. Hornaday,
in the northeast corner of Yellowstone Park.
Part I, Sycamore•Oriole, takes place in 1975,
Part II, Obsidian Point, in 1990, and
Part III, A Season of Poor Tents (the essay), in 1991.

"As I read Ken McCullough's Obsidian Point I said to myself, "I'd love to spend some time out in nature with this guy." As I read on, I realized that I was doing precisely that. McCullough's work has the acute observation, the fine attention to detail, the leisurely pace, the sense of wonder, that only little children or those who have matured into a deep love of nature can know. And the measured and tasted language of the latter. Reading his work, your lungs will expand, your steps will bounce, you will grow hair, and your bones will ache. But it's a good ache."

– Orval Lund

Contents

Acknowledgments 6
Proem 7
PART I 9
  Sycamore • Oriole 11
    Introduction 13
    Comments on Sycamore • Oriole 18
    Daysweat 22
    Ascent 30
    Prelude 35
    Over The Top 38
    Vespers 47
    Night Visitor 49
    Thinking Back To A Peyote Meeting 51
    Late That Spring, Lame Deer 51
    Cloud 57
    Return 60
    Instructions 66
    Notes 67
  Conflagration, September, 1988 68
  Back Country, Yellowstone 69

PART II 71
  Obsidian Point 73

PART III 87
  A Season Of Poor Tents 89
  Coda 106
  Author 108

Acknowledgments

"Proem" appeared in *Rain City Review;*
"Conflagration" appeared in *Slant;*
"Back Country, Yellowstone" and "Obsidian Point" appeared in
Nimrod International Journal;
a section of "Coda" appeared in *No Exit;*
"Thinking Back to a Peyote Meeting" appeared in
The Spirit That Moves Us;
and "Invocation" appeared in *Shaman's Drum;*
"Instructions" appeared in *The Devil's Millhopper* and was
anthologized in
33 Minnesota Poets, Nodin Press (Minneapolis),
and "Vespers" appeared in
Travelling Light (Thunder's Mouth Press, N.Y., 1987).

"Instructions," "Vespers" and "He-Who" were anthologized in
The Ahsahta Anthology: Poetry of the American West
(Boise, Idaho, 1996).

Sycamore • Oriole was first published by The Ahsahta Press, 1991.

Cover painting, oil on canvas by **Lisa Nankivil**
Cover Design by **Nu2 Nugent Design**

Special thanks to the Ucross Foundation, for a residency, and to the Iowa Arts Council, for an Individual Artists Grant, both of which gave me valuable time to work on these and other related pieces.

Proem

1
It was only in the mountains
he was beside himself, inside
himself. In the mountains
he was. And when he prayed
the voice within the boulders
answered. Here was his God,
in the high place, where peace
and fear are married. In
winter, the first forms
breathed for him like stars.

2
A brilliant room in the snow
where only transients may sleep
and the clear water, the water
of eternal life, the stones,
the leaven of forgiveness.
Time takes all who wander in
and reinvents them closer to perfection.

How long he was there, he didn't know,
but he emerged with broken lips.
Brittle junipers began to writhe,
harsh words jumped from umber caves
and a single claw of darkness
raged up at him.

When he came down from there
the locks were changed, the signals
of the body, the songs, the scores.
Houses gone, grottoes rocked over.
Gods had risen in his absence,
others fallen. But he can
ride out any day to the cliffs
of extinction and bring back that dream.

Part I

Sycamore • Oriole

for

Bob Love
Kelly O'Dell
Marie Sanchez
Duncan Galusha

and in memory of
John Woodenlegs

Introduction

Ken McCullough's poetry reminds us of the most basic facts, one of which is that poetry itself, before anything else, is a journey. The journeys that McCullough takes us on are distinctly American ones, treks that guide us down, under, through to the intricate and regenerative lower layers of existence that hide beneath the daily surfaces of our lives, like the crystal lingam ensconced in a deceptively rocklike geode:

>   I scout south along the ridge
>   down the saddle to a shabby weald
>   where, on another trip
>   I found a field of geodes
>   –a crystal lingam
>   ensconced in every one
>   still here by the hundreds
>   the size of coconuts

"Geode": earth-form. For McCullough, the world *is* a geode, a stone with crystal-lined cavities that are accessible only by the kind of penetrating attentiveness that poetry demands. McCullough's journeys, after all, are journeys of language, a rip-rap of words that move us step by step to a dawning realization, the oriole (from "aurora": dawn) in the sycamore.

McCullough's characteristic line in *Sycamore • Oriole* developed from similar shorter works in *Creosote*[1976] and *Travelling Light* [1987] is one that moves the eye around, short ocular journeys back and forth but always and inexorably down. The lines work like water does in the Lao Tzu proverb that opens the book:

>   "Nothing is weaker than water
>   but nothing withstands it
>   nothing will alter its way"

The lines have an insistent flow; they respond immediately and abruptly to any interference, but the jagged flow always arrives at vision: nothing impedes the ultimate descent.

I know of very few poems that prepare readers so carefully for the journeys they are about to take. These are poems of a vision quest, but the vision and the quest require a preparatory regimen, both for the narrator as he hikes deep into the sacred lands of Montana and northern Wyoming, and for the reader whose vision and whose questionings will be trained and tested as the eye follows the I deep into unfamiliar territory. The ocular gradually becomes oracular; the seer as observer gathers his observations into modest prophecy and becomes momentarily a seer of another order.

The most essentially American quest is the peeling off of layers of "civilization" in order to touch the buried spirit of this paved-over land: it is a descent through the palimpsestic layers of American history in order to touch, if only briefly, the savage mystery that this culture has been so intent on forgetting, on denying. The historian Frederick Jackson Turner, in his influential 1893 essay on "The Significance of the Frontier in American History," wrote of how "American social development has been continually beginning over again on the frontier," and how the American character can be understood as a desire for "perennial rebirth" by a "continuous touch with the simplicity of primitive society." Turner portrayed the archetypal American quest as a powerful and irresistible decivilizing transformation:

> The wilderness masters the colonist. It finds him a European in dress, industries, tools, modes of travel, and thought. It takes him from the railroad car and puts him in the birch canoe. It strips off the garments of civilization and arrays him in the hunting shirt and the moccasin.

In *Sycamore • Oriole*, McCullough records and takes us on this same journey of native redefinition:

> off with hiking boots, socks, denims
>   tie on elkhide moccasins
>   –buck naked otherwise
>
> . . .
>   Enter the lodge

These poems take us to earth places where ancient rituals still work, where sage-smoke rubbed on the body can "drain the poisons" from a self that has for too long ingested (and been ingested by) a civilization hell-bent on turning the world to profit: "there is power in the symbols/ though my own faith be weak."

Again and again on these journeys, McCullough arrives at magical spots. These moments never ring false, nor are they arrived at easily: he never abandons the problematics of being a white male Euroamerican trying to imagine his way to a native encounter with the land of his desire. Even at a key moment of unity –

> I stood in the meadow
>   before we whites had come here
>   and felt the pines breathe with me

– a phrase like "we whites" modulates the achievement and quietly acknowledges allegiances that cannot be erased, even as the self feels those allegiances dissipating. Deep in a native sweatbath ritual, McCullough is nonetheless precise and honest (and often funny) about how he is destined to be "a mere pretender/ pseudo-Indian." But such awareness does not preclude a leap of imagination, nor does it preclude learning a new discipline, nor is the attempt to merge natively without efficacy:

>   sweat, snot
> tears, toxins
>   flowing out of me
> I clear my nose
>   backwoods fashion
> Let what is broken, knit!
>   Make the two voices one.

Making the two voices one is every American poet's desire, and McCullough comes close to achieving the impossible melding, to incorporating the tense cultural dialectic into a unified dialect. When the narrator re-emerges into the American cultural present and reverses the stripping off of his civilized clothing –

>   take off lungota
> slip on watch cap, jeans, shirts
>   and high school wrestling sweatshirt

– we experience the conflation of McCullough's American upbringing with the strangeness of native rituals. The "wrestling sweatshirt" has become a sign now of something more than a high school past: the effect of the sweatbaths persists under (and redefines) the sweatshirt, just as the body's memory of the lungota remains beneath the jeans, and the narrator will now wrestle with the attempt to live both lives, to dress in two cultures. Back down from his spiritual journey up Mount Hornaday, he knows he has been to a very different "high" school ("This place was my teacher, my Marpa," McCullough writes in a recent poem about Hornaday [Part II, "Obsidian Point"]), has sweated for a different set of purposes, and has learned he must now wrestle opponents unlike any he has faced before. Once the re-dressed body has been stripped and put through a set of ancient rituals, it must wear its old familiar clothes in an unfamiliar way; the identical clothes no longer signal the same identity.

So, when the narrator climbs Mount Hornaday in his "un-Injun" fashion, he realizes

>   . . . you can set yr sights
> surprise yrself
>   at yr
>   pilgrim's progress

The "yr" is part of McCullough's dialect of ease and informality (working) to de-form and re-form and in-form the shape of the poem), but this slangy abbreviation – "your" trimmed to "yr"– also neatly captures a   cleaning out of a part of the self, turning the self lean, emptying the vowels, ridding the self of selfishness, a ritual of purgation, surprising yourself by discovering the ur-self that offers a unified base, a centered point of light around which "you can set yr sights" and begin yr progress.

The vision quest in this book – the mystical encounter with bear, rattler, and bull elk, with chipmunks, chickadees, and butterflies – are finally in the service not of a retreat to the past (to be "the first to step here/ in 100 years"), but rather of a life lived in the present. The sacred and remote landscapes in these poems open finally onto the secular and the familiar; the piss firs and chickadees yield the sycamore and oriole. If the journeys recorded in this book were initially withdrawals precipitated by the death of McCullough's father and the absence of his son, the journeys work through loss and guide McCullough back to renewed relationships with both father and son, lead him to the mystery of generation(s), to the discovery of the centered "path of light" that passes from father to son – the "stream of light" that, like the water, brooks no interference:

>   . . . I see behind his black eyes

> my own son, his grandson
> and a path of light opens
> running through the three of us

Sycamore • Oriole concludes with a stunningly lyrical pentameter set of instructions to McCullough's son, yielding the fruit of his journeys. They are directions to a place where there are no dams, to a place where his son might hold his own ground, where he must learn to "Breathe. Speak sharply." In this book, McCullough teaches himself – and all who are lucky enough to read him– the same lesson. On this journey you will travel light, and to light.

> *Ed Folsom*
> Iowa City, Iowa
> June, 1991

Comments on Sycamore • Oriole

"*Sycamore • Oriole* is a book rooted in respect and understanding for the natural landscape which all too many American poets have used as nothing more than a backdrop for their own angst. There's a quiet understanding in each of these poems which never crosses over into conceit and is balanced by the sort of understated humor which I've always admired in some of Gary Snyder's best work. Like a walk in the wilderness, this sequence of poems takes you out to the edge of civilized vision and – if you listen closely enough – lets you see a ways beyond, hear some of the old wild songs of danger and exultation which are always there."
– Joe Bruchac

"Attentive to both the human and non-human universe, and humorously humble in its stance toward them both, Ken McCullough's record of climb and descent is a fine corrective antidote to the numerous pre-packaged 'vision quests' cluttering the shelves of New Age bookstores.

Even to a decadent city slicker like myself – who has spent many years now in towns surrounded by the wide open spaces he read about as a kid in the novels of Karl May and Zane Gray – this narrative of mountains, glaciers, and sweat lodge visions shines with a similar aura of adventure, daring and persistence, while being quite a bit more believable and in tune with intelligent wistful late twentieth-century sensibility."
– Anselm Hollo

"McCullough builds a sweat lodge of words, heating up a fire that purifies and endures."
–Diane Glancy

"This is no ordinary group of longish poems concerned with one man's meditative wanderings in several parts of the high country of Montana and Wyoming. I say it is not ordinary, because there are many such collections, and they are ordinary. The attempt to find one's self in a world that denies self is a laudable one, but it often ends up with an A for effort. Not so these poems, which in a leisurely swinging stride attempt to forge a ritual which is personal but deeply rooted in the past of the earlier ones who moved through this same high country, as well as in the past of many other traditions. The ritual itself is no mere collage – it comes through the process of the poems. That is what, more than any other single factor, sets them apart from the ordinary. They are poems that could be left on the bark and leaves of that country, or could be carried into other countries / contexts by anyone receptive to the search for what is always around us, but which many deny. I can't be moved by these poems in the way that Ken McCullough is, but I am moved, and I recommend the experience, each in his own way, to other readers of this fine clear book. I can hope that there will be many such, and for a long time."
– Theodore Enslin

"The language of gender shapes this new volume of poetry by Ken McCullough, recording a series of journeys, literal as well as metaphorical, into western wilderness to summon the spirit of place and experience union with it; in doing so, to heal estrangements in his life as seeker, lover, father, son.

The kind of journey the poet makes is seen by Ed Folsom, writing in the Introduction, as 'the most essentially American quest... peeling off... layers of this paved-over land... a descent through the palimpsestic layers of American history in order to touch, if only briefly, the savage mystery that this culture has been so intent on forgetting, on denying.'"...

Thoreau only wrote of making an offering to the ancient powers he sensed all around him on Mt. Katahdin, but McCullough enters his places prepared to do just that... All the past experiences which have sent McCullough into the mountains are embedded in fragments of memory or longing or hallucination. The poetry is tough climbs, of balancing on narrow ridges while one's eye sucks in vistas. Of the smell of mountain meadows, of sleeping on rock, and the exertion and

exhilarating mind pull of striding across the backbone of the continent....The prose rhythms and man-style roughness convey very well the gritty, self-contained work of the solitary hiker and those moments when a sudden sliding rock or a cracking twig prickle the neck hairs with cold awareness of having trod a domain more ancient and arcane even than rings of stone."
    The Redneck Review of Literature

These events took place outside Bozeman, Montana,
near Lame Deer, Montana
and on Mount Hornaday, northwest Wyoming
in late September 1975.

Dayswaet

breeze
    just getting up
        in canyons to the south
  slow silver strands
      streaming from the aspen
    leaves twitter
        a week from their yellow swansong
     in the clearing
        brittle ribcage
       overgrown with thistles —
sixteen willow branches
      bent to form a frame
   red, white and black
          bands of horsehair
     bind the joints
   stand of horsemint
       rings the center hole
char
   at the roots of the thistles
        door due east
     clots of sodden elkhide
          where we used to sit
I haul bulky tarps
      and drape them on the frame
     mildewed canvas/ smell of childhood
         check for light leaks
    crawling
       in the womb-dark place

at the miner's sluice
      fill bucket with glacier run-off
          minnows tremble in formation

        in reflection
     of ferns on the other bank
       "Nothing is weaker than water
but nothing withstands it
           nothing will alter its way"

🍂

break off
    dead cottonwood branch
  the heartwood
      a five-pointed star
    —symbol of the Great Spirit
place the tinder
    four sticks on top of it
      running east-west
   four north-south
     stack the rest in a cone
  moving   as the sun   moves
      place rocks at the cardinal points
        then pile the rest
    kneel
      facing east
   light the tinder
and watch
    the Shape-Changer's
   cautious tongues
off with hiking boots, socks, denims
    tie on elkhide moccasins
  —buck naked otherwise
     Tote logs from back of camper
        rasp of bark on arms and chest
       stoke the blaze
      singeing arm hairs
          to tight black wires

🍂

Enter the lodge
   bundle of sage
  in one hand
     buckskin
         pouch in the other
   crawl around center hole
           clockwise
    as the sun   moves

                spread sage on my spot
              and sit by the bucket
                   full-lotus
            drop cluster of sage on the embers
         thick   smoke
                    sharp   dry
                 the scent of a woman
                         from the high desert
                 catches my breath
                       my eyes water   nose runs
                 With cupped hands
                         take the smoke
                     and pass it over my head
         brush over arms, legs and torso
                     to drain the poisons from me

         take out
              poke of kinikinik
                     of sweet Ann root
                mixed with Half&Half
              tamp into old briar
                      light up with ropey stem of sage
                 this smoke
                      sharpens the focus
             and no three-day carcass breath

         a pinch to the west rains
              the north winds
            the east—sun/light, fertility and knowledge
               south—the womb and tomb of life
                      the heavens
                          the earth
                to yours truly

         Grand/mother
                 when this, my flesh
                        feeds crows and blowflies
                and the bones are bleached
                         and scattered in the sun
                 leave
                    a stand of mint to mark the spot
                 or if I fall in marshy ground
                        let me
                     become a bed of watercress
         I feel you here, faintly

                    Come to me!
            You have cast your net
                        over all your creatures
        but I fear
            snares and nets
                Help me!
            I know
                what I believe
                but do not
        believe what I know

            the rocks
                glow orange
            spit   dances on them
                            evaporates
                With forked limb
                        roll them
                            into center hole
sweat
    stings my eyes

I crawl through the flap
    ass in the air
        balls swinging
    in the four-legged darkness
        no fear of it
    but sometimes I want to stay here

Dip sage in bucket
            swatch the rocks
    which hiss back at me
                violently
        steam rises
        fills the lodge
            and a wave of sweat
            sloughs from my body

"Only one who takes upon himself
                the evils of the world
        may be its king"
    I, no king— a mere pretender
        pseudo-Indian
                slumped inside my own emotions

                begin to weep—
                        sweat, snot
                tears, toxins
                        flowing out of me
                I clear my nose
                        backwoods fashion
                Let what is broken, knit!
                        Make the two voices one!

... my son
        delicate nostrils
                puffing easily
   in deep sleep
            stretches
        snuggles like a bearcub
        tiny beads of sweat
            on the bridge of his nose...

not for myself alone
        but that I might become
      a fit instrument
            to bring back news
    to him, to your other children
            that they might not spend their souls
  ... but *Thy* will, *Thy* will
            be done

let me
    follow the blazes
    read the spoor
            and when I hear your wings
        overhead in the night
                    smell your shadow
                watching me
                        from a grove of lodgepole
        do not let me
                run in sleep
            but turn to face you
    hear you say
            "This is my beloved son
                    of whom I am very skeptical
            I will not let him
                    rest in still waters
        until he walks these parapets
        with his eyes closed

    and sees by the light
      that shines within him"

🪶

I chant in a high falsetto
   no meaning to the syllables
 a mindless song
   the song goes flat
 old weary distant
the energy soughs off
  my son, his mother
  my weakness darkness
    I am not worthy to receive you
  but only say the word
    and I shall be healed
   maybe
  if I stay on this path
     to the next promontory

strip off
gray-green leaves of sage
   and rub them on my body
  drop them on the rocks
 May this smell
    cleanse all those above, around
   and beneath me here
  may this smell
    bite back into all of us
   living here on you, Mother

The steam losing its power
    feel for the handle
  tip bucket on the rocks
    inhale a double hit
  and let it
    fill my sinuses
  a hoarse growl
    involuntary
 issues from my chest
   as I fight passing out
    When it passes
 I sprawl to the doorflap
  my head through the entrance
   I have to squint

```
                against the brilliance
no feeling in the left leg
            pinpricks
       as blood
            surges through constricted vessels
      I have to crawl
              using my elbows
When I am out
       push to a standing position
                    and stagger up the path
            —though it's 80⁰
                 I shiver uncontrollably
      foot and leg buzzing with feeling
              crabwalk up the bank
        grab a stump and
               swing down in the sluice
         up to the waist
                     ice rush
       balls shrink up inside my body
foreskin there for a reason
             push off and fall backwards
         with Bonzai yell
      totally immersed
               shocks jerk head out of water
         snorting    blowing     snarling
  thrash a bit, then
           haul myself out

              clamber up the bank
   and stand there
          arms raised    reborn
                not a birth in terror and pain
        but each dwindling cell
               replaced
       I scan the Bridgers
                purple and gray
          through an ancient golden light
     across the valley as it was
                     5,000 years ago
     this water ringing down
            taste it
       see it sparkle as it did then
     the tastes the smells the sounds
                fill my body taut
            I stand
```

                    naked before you
              humble but not ashamed
                          the neighbor's chainsaw
                        snarling in the timber
ready

              ready to begin

Ascent

head north
    on trail that follows Pebble Ck.
      bushwhack off
  toward sheer face of Hornaday
         into same shady meadow
    last summer/ full of King Boletus
     — big white heads
    some beginning to redden
       a little salt a little butter
       the biggest
           a meal for two
pick up game trail
     other side of meadow
    entrance guarded this July by
         large fly Amanita
   blood red cap as big as my fist
    white warts on its surface
  like bits of cottage cheese
        —from a distance
   a cartoon sesame bun
but don't eat this one
   Initiation rite of shamans in Siberia—
eat seven of them
    fall into the underworld
and be hacked apart by a raging dwarf
   (same height as a mushroom)
  the proposition, then
     to find the parts and
  put yourself together again
    before you surface
      to the conscious world
never eat them raw
   or cooked up fresh
      The shamans
    dried them like chilies
      softened them up by chewing
  then swallowed them whole
     When the cache ran low
   had a fellow
     partaker
    piss in yr cup

                        held yr nose
and swilled it down
            the buzz
                still strong
symptoms: nausea, barfing
                thirst enough to drain an ocean
    blue skin and foaming at the mouth
                blindness, visions
        non-stop babbling
                singing and marionette twitching
        able to
            swing a full-grown yak
                over yr head by its tail
set off
    in the dead of winter
    and run non-stop to the next village
        50 miles upriver
and get there
            yesterday
some say
        the cult
            crept across the boondocks
    to Norway
            Berserkers
            stoked up on them
                    before they stormed the battlefield
            —they "went berserk"
not so, say the acid scholars
                fly Amanita the same
                        Soma of the Rig Veda
                rarely leads to violence

its cousin
    the Destroying Angel
                more lethal
            symptoms
                sometimes a day late
        then

your body turns to stone
                from the outside in

but they live East of here

        (never eat a white Amanita)

    on up the trail
        a few distant relatives
      leathery, distorted
            some inkly blue
        some bruise-purple

easy going now
    on moss-and-needle matting

up through the trees
      huge cloudbank on Hornaday
      squatting like a shy old invertebrate
        unwilling, unable to move
      just a wisp of it
          spills over a cliff
another sign of autumn

🝆

trail dips at a little crik   patch of sunlight
    I kneel
        balancing backpack
  and suck in water
    cold enough to make my teeth ache
At the back of my neck
      feeling of being watched
  I look up
    slowly

—in shadow
  on the other bank
    a ten-point whitetail
      broadside
    its head turned toward me
eyes dark with curiosity
      nostrils flex
  as its scents me
        flies buzz round its head
      our eyes stay on each other
    then it raises its rack
  haughtily
    prances off through the trees
      without looking back

🝆

pick pale yellow

                    coral mushroom
                from backside of aspen
                    nip off a bit   peppery taste
            Before I'd come out West
                            I'd never eaten mushrooms
                    not even storebought ones
                            —tidy Anglo-Saxon bugaboo
            against the toad's stool

                            I'd travelled light before
                    on other treks up Hornaday
                        packed no food—
            cooked up cinquefoil roots, cow's parsnips
                            dandelion greens, ate berries
            This alpine flora—
                    unless you eat things
                    when they're ripe—
                            is either toxic
                                or tastes like tripe
                        —alpine huckleberries
                            will send you to yr bed
                            if you eat them when they're red
            —fruit of
                one of the lilies
                a cherry tomato
                            lookalike
            is tart and pleasant
                    when it's bright red
                otherwise
                    the game-day trots

                but why food at all?

                Giri Bala, India
            on aether, sun and air
            Therese Neumann, Bavaria
                    40 years
                    on a consecrated host a day

            faith, me heartee
                    for *this* vessel
                    to dine on fare so spare

            🐟

            climbing now

           the trail rockier
     frequent stops to catch my breath
            and glimpse
                  ubiquitous chickadees
         zipping in and out

scare up a blue grouse
                  roar of its wings
snaps me
     back to center

it's starting to get dark

         water break
     at stream of ropey lace
  cascading down moss
                 rockface

            last water
               before I come down the mountain

off to the right
       I hear a waterfall
       I go that way
           across the grain of the ravines
       finally give up the idea
            and climb straight up
              breaking off a sturdy limb
                      from a dead piss fir
             to use as an extra leg
         —straight up is un-Injun

                   but you can set yr sights
             surprise yrself
           at yr
                 pilgrim's progress

Prelude

   a few feet off the trail
         deep slashes on a big tree
      ten feet up—
        bear with the highest marks
    claims the territory
'tis   a griz

    pop of twigs
      as herd of elk
         gallops into the dusk

  wind shifts   the smell of water
       sweet water
         fills my nostrils
   and then wild roses
      a whole valley full of them
comes to life in the evening's air
      but too late in the year for roses

      I notice
        a circle of stones sunk
    into the ground—
        a wickiup ring
    left by the Sheepeaters
a good spot, then—
    other moccasins have worn
the ground smooth here
   a hundred years before

the equinox—
   maybe the Old Ones
      will come out
    and dance around me in a circle
       la noche encantada

🐻

in a fold of
   meditation blanket
     in the backpack

   hoisted up a tree
a small pouch—
   my son's umbilicus, a scraper
    obsidian bird points
& five claws from the left front paw
    of a black bear

coming down from Hornaday
     on another trek
  got in some loose rock
and braced myself
  to keep from sliding off a cliff
hand
  fell on this paw, intact
    attached to ulna and radius
   from which the flesh was stripped
    —no other bones around
(after the berries dry up in August
   griz go after blacks)
with my Buck knife
   I sawed off
     the desiccated paw
  and packed it out

    down near Mt. Langford
  a griz followed me for two hours
    never saw or heard him
  just the stink of sulfur

Moon full tonight
   sleep only in short spells
  waking up
    to follow the shifting firmament
   snuggle down with head inside the bag
and sink in easy sleep

🐾

A heavy weight across my body
  Am I dreaming No.
   I want to give the weight
a left jab or forearm shiver
   but the grunt stops me—
  cross between
   grunt and insistent idiot whine

A lot of good the hatchet
                out there on the ground

The beast
    fumbles through my stuff
        but why stretched out across me?
    my scent has spooked it
                not one iota
        Finally it gives up
    lifts its bulk
        by pushing on my chest
            with front paws as it rises
        goes over
            to where the pack hangs
& lets loose a burst of sad complaints
        before it moves
            up the hillside

When it's gone
    I untie the bow to my bag
            and poke my head out—
        in the moonlight
            see its silhouette
        two-year old   male
    No grizzly
        but glad I hadn't
                given it a shot
trapped inside my mummy bag

    twice my weight   still bawling

            I take
        three draughts of sharp mountain air
        and settle back
            into the cool nylon bag

            —an outward and visible sign
        and all's right with the world

hang onto yr hat, bucko

Over The Top

birds wake me
   up and on my way in minutes
     grasping
        scrubby
            mountain mahogany
     juniper
       twisted in human shapes
and on and up
   for three hours pushing it
until I recognize
      palisades rimming crest of Hornaday
   scramble to the top
     & pile some stones
   to mark my way back down
           over the edge of the world

the top of Hornaday
   laid our like a golfcourse
   in Scotland of the imagination
   open, rocky, trim
     with lots of natural hazards
   but here
pterodactyls glide in for amphibious landings
      on the sheep wallow ponds
     pristine in the distance

benchmark says
   MT. HORNADAY ELEV. _____ FT.
    —close enough fr guv'mint work

     on the flat at last
   center my backpack
     and step out randy as a goat
      bearbell dinging
  singing a Hank Snow medley
    incipient blisters
    sighing "Hallelujah!
     We shall be released!"

to my right
    up ahead
 a small butte
  where I'll find my power spot
     in the *krummholz,* the "fairy woods"—
piss firs dwarfed and fused in grottoes
  where elves and other small ones live:
the small hard wind-twisted
  Sheepeaters
    hair sawed off with odsidian
   straight across like Incas
    hunkered at a fire
      with the best view around
chipping at feathery
  almost transparent bird points

 around one boulder
  I always come upon a man
       mummified
   yellow-brown skin
  varnished across his grin
   some wisps of blanket stuck to him
    reclining
in the posture
where he'd sat to dream
  some 90 years ago

🐾

deposit backpack
  at base of bluff
 slow circuit of the meadow
     then sidehill to the top

  the east edge—
   a broken line
     of piss fir and limber pine
    the rest bare
     except for scattered boulders
      dropped in hasty retreat—
    not hard to imagine
      dinosaurs in the valley below
   to their shoulders in sulfured mists
    and why the Crow thought it

       haunted
     and up near Three Forks
    —Logan, to be exact
      stumps of palm trees
     petrified

I scout south along the ridge
     down the saddle to a shabby weald
   where, on another trip
I found a field of geodes
    —a crystal lingam
      ensconsed in every one
still here by the hundreds
the size of coconuts

     back up the ridge to a spot
       on the edge of the bluff
    almost where I'd emerged
       when I'd sidehilled up
    —elf grove
      five yards behind
     on either side

  sit   rest

   the two ponds to one side
   below me

  mountains 360^0

I have lived here five years:
   a distance in my eyes now—
  a puffiness in my face—
    the detritus of knowledge
   has settled in
but still no wisdom
  and the boyhood grace
  has blown away
    leaving cracked bedrock

   I get up and saunter
  to the north end of the ridge
     steep drop-off
  Cut-off Peak in the midground
   slumped like a heathen fortress
      disguised as Birnham Wood

                    this end of the bluff
                            somehow impoverished

                    then back to my spot
                and clatter down through loose rock
                                    & grasshoppers
                    to retrieve my gear

                        the hairs on my neck
                tell me

                            this is the place

🐾

from buckskin shoulder bag
        take paper sack of cornmeal
        ground in handmill at home
            scrape the loose gravel
                        around with my boot
            smooth out an eight-foot circle
                dribble cornmeal
            in a scrawny trail around the edge
                clockwise, to keep out the uninvited
            —there is power in the symbols
                        though my own faith be weak

I decide that
    after I've settled in
        I won't step beyond the circle
        'til the course is run—
        This won't be
    no overnight conversion, though—
I am Cancer (hard shell
            hard sell)
        born a Baptist and guilty
            until proven otherwise
    If They want me
        They'll have to earn it

piss around the circle's edge
            to mark my territ'ry
        presumptuous, perhaps
        (Mr. Griz
                my friends remind
        won't pay no nevermind
                to *that* particular etiquette)

            but Moccasin Joe
                  (ole Juan Osa)
            my friend and brother—
he knows
   he'll find no Luger in my gear

     break off piss fir boughs
     for mattress on the pebbly skin—
        with each branch
          pitch handful of cornmeal
at base of the trunk
       leave trace in the pouch
      for the unexpected

take out large buckskin bag
        stuffed with sage
              picked down near Gardiner
    unlace it
      scatter sage on my sitting place
        spread the groundcloth
roll out the sleeping bag
      backpack for a backrest
     off with the Frankenstein boots
and lay socks out
       for sweat to evaporate

     fringe of crusty snow
        on shadow of an elf grove—
claw out a handful and
       rub it on the soles of my feet
      then my forehead
     stinging my brain alive

       chronic aches
        run straight through —
        too many spirits
             of the fifth kind
    too many lifetimes
     strip off the denim shirt and jeans
       put jockstrap
in outer pocket of the backpack—
     naked, now   in the middle
    of everywhere
unfold Chinese-red lungota

                loop it snugly between my legs
                        and wind it around my abdomen
                    —erection rears its surly head
                            tie on elkhide moccasins, again
                red bandanna around my forehead...
                    If a Parkie trailcrew
                                wanders through
                    and finds me in this getup...
                            but this ain't Grand Central
                    and the trails
                            kept up by deer, elk, sheep
and Bigfeet

                I bow in the six directions
            sink to the cold nylon
                        doubled to form a cushion
                    facing East
                            two o'clock
                        shut my eyes
and fall out into long slow breathing

an old farmhouse   an orchard
            three towheads
        swooping in like swallows
                when they're called to dinner
        fading   fading

            fingers meshed in a socket
                    in front of my crotch
                my erect penis strains against the red cloth
                    with my left hand
                            lightly palpate my testicles
            tightened against my body
                —will there be
                        any other progeny?

        then, in an hour
        the shadow of a tree
                    touches my right knee
                and the temp change brings me
            to the surface

I chant spontaneous
    Shrii Ram, Jai Ram

     Jai Jai, Ram Om
 in a clear tenor
   so resonant
    my skullbones buzz
 on the verge of pain

within a minute
  a dozen chickadees
   flutter down and light
     on a small boulder
  a few feet from me
I can see
the energy in their eyes
  their sharp little tongues
 they twitch and flap
    with a steady tweeping—
  my voice's frequency
 has crossed their wires
    it draws them to me
  but they don't know why
or what to do

I chant until my cords
  have come unstrung
 and when I stop
     the silence

  —in an instant
   the chickadees are gone

 a few wisps in the sky—
don't be misled

  up this way
   She'll lure you do you in —
  while you're in there shooting stick
   and swilling rotgut
    She'll drop it down to 35 below
  If you skid off the road
 in a snowbank three miles from home
they'll find you in the morning—
  oblivion
   will have sailed
deep inside your eyes

    Except for June through August
        I keep a mummy bag
                stuffed behind the seat
       —if you flirt with Her
              be ready

Should I take this gear
    stuff it in the backpack
        pitch it into space
    then see what happens?

I once picked up a hitchhiker
    who wore just a pair of shorts—
        no gear, no money
             and a sunburned grin
        on his way to Seattle
        from Bangor, Maine
a part of me
    wants to be

  that free

In a week I'll leave this life behind me
    my son, his mother—
        to a new job, the ocean, palmettos
            and graceful women
  the drone note will
        dissipate, I hope
but diaspora
   fouls the corners of my vision—
   for this next act
 play it as yourself, friend
        STRANGE LANDS AND SEPARATION
            ARE THE STRANGER'S LOT
    "A wanderer has no fixed abode;
        his home is the open road.
    Therefore he must take care
        to remain upright and steadfast,
           so that he sojourns only in the proper places
          associates only with good people
       that he has good fortune
          and can go his way unnoticed."

 🌂

late in the afternoon

        take off lungota
     slip on watch cap, jeans, shirts
  and high school wrestling sweatshirt
          sit again in meditation
peek with one eye
              at chipmunk
                sneaking up the bluff
    hiding behind small boulders
      comes within a few feet
                nibbling corn meal
  closer, it stands on its haunches
                    worrying weed seed from a stalk
        near edge of ground cloth
     then, with bold eyes
              hops on my knee
                    scurries up my arm to my shoulder
        and sniffs at my ear
              —all I can do to keep from barking
   at those tiny claws
           on bare skin
—curiosity satisfied
     he scoots over side of the bluff

Vespers

due South, through a gap
    the Tetons
        just of hip, full breast
la grande teton
        I can hear
    the song of flowers   driven inward
  deep in the cells   a death without complication
    to the west   smoked broken quartz
      intense peach at the horizon
            floating up to pale lavender
      two camprobbers
    vop voop voop in for a landing
        strut   squawk   looking for a handout
      adjourn in brisk jay fashion
to the east   Abiathar and The Thunderer
      stained deep indigo
  Venus appears
    in the crack
    between sundown and moonrise
a coyote yips
    and his younger brother reports
      deliberate   on the breaths   a meditation
    in a week
      I could break that code
an elk from another planet
      bugles for his mate
  and the wind comes up
    as the moon
      pokes its dome over the mountains
    by now   above me
the Bear rides low in the sky
    looking for a place to hibernate
    the Hunting Dogs yapping at his heels
      Mizar his eye
        at the bend of the Dipper
    and Alcor, its companion
          barely visible
(the "human beings" knew them as
      the Horse and Rider)
    the diamond of Delphinus
        forms Job's Coffin
    Aldeberan

                    the Bull's eye
          Cygnus
                    hangs there as the Northern Cross
               These designs—
                         mariners and shepherds
                              what else to do
                         with their time at night?
     a shooting star   another
                    and a third
                         so close I expect to hear it
                    then a small bright object
                         steadily across the sky —
                    a satellite
               you can tell the time by
     As the stars loom closer
                    an electric hum
                              like distant crows
          I am falling up to
               a huge necropolis
                         lit by torches
               my breath   swarms the moonlight
                    and I start to chant:
     I do not presume to come to this
                    Thy table, Mother
                         without my knife in my boot
               I must make my choice
                    before the wall of ice falls away
          If you ask me
               can I identify insanity for you
                    I'd have to say
                         I've explored the mainland
                    but my maps might be
                              too particular
                    like the divine geometry
               you've etched on my fingertips
                    I travel this new road
                              because I want to
                         though I do not feel
                    or see where it leads
               let it be
                    on this side of the river
               let the snow
               with its simple thirst
                         take time to invent my fragrance

Night Visitor

    the moon comes up
        long shadow of myself
    on the ground in front of me
        chanting
    up and down the scale
    the tide rolls in
            inside me
  something moving
        in the loose rock behind
      larger than a scamperer
          not bear elk or coyote
      unless the chant
          has lured them
I do not turn and look
  safe
 within the syllables
the shadow of something else
         at the edge of my own
    I keep on chanting
        though every muscle tightens
   now the shadow
      takes on definition
           obscures my own
I chant   I do not turn
  I can see behind me
      without turning—

 there
    two feet away
coiled   and ready to strike
    the largest rattler
        I have ever seen
   flat triangular head
      poised three inches
   above the level of my own
       slightly swaying
   the black beads of its eyes
smell of
   ripe cucumbers
      tongue   flicks in and out
        it is coiled   but not rattling
      I gaze straight ahead
    this   beyond me

                    I chant more loudly
                hoping for protection

            What is it
                    I have called up?
                twelve feet long
                        big around as one of my thighs
        —no rattlers above 4,000 feet
                but this at 10,000
            and out in the open
                        this time of night

I look in the eyes again
        just as it rears its head
    imperceptibly
                and strikes
                    the top of my head—
        flash of white
                    incandescent light
    as it forces
        down   into my body
                through the opening
        it has made   in the
                    crown of my skull
            its body
            coursing   into my body
                    one great muscular
                            pouring in
pushed
            pushed to my outermost walls

            finally
                I disappear

    . . . an hour later
            by the turning of the heavens
        I return
            sitting in a half-lotus
    right where I had been

Thinking Back To A Peyote Meeting Late That Spring, Lame Deer

Jasper

Jasper Crazy Woman's face
had been split with an ax, then
put back together kittywumpus.
Though he came late to the meeting
they made room for him up front.
His neighbor tuned the skin with extra care
before he drummed for him.
When Jasper sang, the voice was high
and flat like an Okie woman
at a Pentecostal hymnsing.
His eyes looked up and out.
His song stitched itself acoss
the years of my aloneness
and it fell out like fine sand.
Most sang for fifteen minutes
before the drum was passed
but Jasper wheeled out into the night
to look inside his people
one by one.

Invocation

The name of Jesus Christ
    would wander through a song
  but otherwise
      the language was Cheyenne.
    After Jasper sang
  the second time
      the roadman
   asked me why.
To have my family back, I said,
    that you pray for me
       to be strong, to wait.
    And they did. I sank down
        and wept and the prayers
      circled over the embers
    and they glowed like the
        heart of the world.
   We   are your   *family*
    We are   your heart your heart

Then I went out
  into the darkness
    under the crooked signs.
I stood in the meadow
    before we whites had come here
  and felt the pines breathe with me.
A sadness, a sadness, a sadness
    echoed to my depths.
  The pain of life was splitting me.
    The teepee behind me
     shimmered
       and the songs within
    lit the stars
    like ice.

You are the guest here,
              not the taker—
    no judge,
        not even of yourself
I knew I didn't have to
    but I went back in. Now,
my own life, every mistake
        each lie, and mean spirit
    marched up before me. Leave me!
            end it!   get out!   save yourself!

Brothers

Just before the sun came up
odd croaks outside the teepee.
The doorman raised the flap and
two deaf brothers in their sixties
moved clockwise round the circle.
They sat in the place we made
to the right of the roadman.
For the next eternity
he spoke to them in sign—
long stories that others
now and then would add to.
And jokes that made the circle
bray like goats and donkeys.
The deaf men's laughs were wheezes.
I laughed, too, but only twice
did I have the slightest clue.

He - Who

Whenever I looked
he was staring straight at me
one eye ablaze.
The fat woman next to me
chortled—
she knew the score.
I asked her
to nudge me when his guard was down.
In a few minutes
her elbow grazed me
but just as I flicked my eyes
his way
he was locked on me.
The fat woman
insisted I take more powder—
like trying to swallow
the pulverized
bones of your ancestors.
I got sick—
nothing much came up
but the fat woman
gave me a grin
knowing this bit of humility
would make me less
an observer.
The doorman came with a shovel
and scooped up
what I'd disgorged.
So the night went on—
I'd look up
and he'd have his eye on me.
Finally the light came
through the wall of the teepee
and the smoke turned bright blue
and we broke the fast—
dried corn, some meat
that was pretty rich
spring water

and fruit cocktail.
We went outside
and I wandered
five feet up
with a brittle grin on my face.
"What kind of meat was that?"
I asked the roadman.
"Do you remember that black Lab pup
you were playing with last week?"
That dropped me down a foot or two.
Then I looked for my nemesis—
no sign of him.
The fat woman nodded up a knoll
toward an aspen grove.
A figure curled up in a blanket.
I sneaked up, quiet
in my moccasins
and came around the figure.
It was he, looking up at me
with that incendiary eye.
Later, the fat woman told me his name:
He-who-sleeps-with-one-eye-open.

Cloud

the axis of the sun
    runs straight through me
I am
 half man
half other
   beside myself
  each breath
     takes place
  this place
   as its home
      I look
    straight ahead
 a white blur undulates
      at the edge of my vision
small cloud of moths or butterflies
     given the frantic nature of their flight
    the swarm moves
   across the flat below me
butterflies, small ones, thousands
    light on the hillside
   just beneath my spot
     a few mavericks still flutter above me
 their wings brown ochre, dove-gray
   with an eye on each
  pale yellow stripe   an ivory band
    they are settled now
 though one might drift like a mote
   they flex their wings
      straight up   in unison
     in slow pulses
    I've seen a gaggle of cabbage moths
     chase hilarious
       across a clover field
    but never such a congregation
though they do not touch
   the song they listen to
  is clear and sweet
   but too benign for mating
I sit

      in this delicate grace
    and tears roll down
          through the parched valley of my face

❧

as quick as their descent
      they arise *en masse*
     across the surface of the ponds
and down the lip of the mountain
        I follow them out of sight
     then notice the ground
      and the grass around me
everywhere they've been
   is spotted red
     droplets even on my clothes
      I touch one
       as thick as blood
   and taste it
     bitter   sharp
a shiver up my spine
   the bones of my skull
         ring
           like thin crystal
    as the light comes in
the sky-prow
    parts the curtain
and I see you
   standing
      in your heavy clothes
  the breath in your nostrils
   visible
      in the midday air

❧

sitting again—
   pass the rudraksha beads
      twixt thumb and index finger

   the sweet air
      washes over me
    and I am adrift
      until I sense someone

and the smell of meat gone bad
    I turn my head
           slowly
—there behind me
              rack down
is a bull elk
      trained on me—
afraid that he might charge
           I push myself to him
      through my eyes
his head stops bobbing
            as if to listen—
    takes two steps toward me
      paws three times
          with his right front hoof
    and canters away

Return

    clamber over the rim
        head light as cottonwood down
            so take it slow
  —in the loose rock
    the first marker
        placed there on the way up
      in case I'd become disconnected
I wouldn't strike off
        in a wide demented circle
      until they came in after me
   I could step off into the air
soar like that eagle
    on a thermal there
    above Mt. Norris

   I gain speed as I rumble downward
        —forget about the markers
    these feet
      with minds of their own
        I give them full rein
   half-run half-glissade
      I land on a goat trail
        that winds along a ledge
    trail splits and my feet
say switchback—
   the direction we just came
   hollow nimble goatman
    I hear
      the waterfall I couldn't find
     on the way up
and then I scamper under it
    as it cascades out over the trail
      the spray hits my face
absolute   perfect
  but it doesn't
     interrupt my pace

          around next bend of the trail
                    a cave
               slopes back 20 feet in the rock
                    two long shelves
                  chipped into the wall

     a quiet here I've never felt before
               I could   be here forever

                    on one wall
                         the silhouette on gray rock
                                   of a faint black hand
          Time curls on itself in a corner
                                   and sleeps.
               A man sang to a woman here
                    and they died. A man's secrets
                    in the powdered earth—
                         powder so light
                              it hovers in a cloud
                    around my feet
                    —in the dirt a stick
          with carved designs
     all but obliterated:
                    porcupines had nibbled
               the surface smooth—
                    a Sheepeater place

          I am the first to step here
          in 100 years—
     when I know
          my time has come
          I will steal to this place again
               be
                    redistrubuted
          a death
          with no supporting cast

 I stretch out on my back
                    cool in the cave
               slight chill as the sweat
     evaporates from my skin—
                    pillowed in the dust

      I look in the tops of the trees
  and feel someone moving along the trail
    a shape shifts into the shadow
        no anguish in his face at last:
    my silent father

                *

        home for the last time
     I glassed the trees
with the new binoculars he'd brought from Vietnam
    he joined me
        waiting for me to begin
  but I did not
He said "Do you see that o-riole
               up there?"
    I said "No, where is it?"
    "Up in that big sickymore."
  I went through the motions
     of focusing on the oriole
    too ashamed to admit
      I had no idea
        what a sycamore looked like

  we stood there
    he waiting
   me unable to speak
then I excused myself—
    important calls to make

    in my room
      I looked out the window
  saw him bend
    to the soil of his garden
crumble a handful in his large fingers
    hold it to his nose
        and smell its richness—
  his eyes were closed

      the next time I saw him
        he was in his casket

*

      I tell him that when he
          left his body
              we were both broken, beyond repair
           but his visits to my dreams
                have helped to heal us
in one dream
   in Grandma's front parlor, Staten Island
        (maternal side)
     we are all assembled
Christmas, probably
    dressed in the styles of the late 40's
          post-war optimistic, laughing
      getting ready to go out visiting
my father is relaxed, cracking jokes
         suddenly, he pitches to the floor
       holding his chest
            —we all know what this means
   Mom becomes hysterical
      he calls to her
         asks her, please, to be calm
I kneel next to him
    and cradle his head
      the sweet smell of witch hazel on his face
     he looks as he did
the day he took me to see Ole Miss
    play 'Bama, with Connerly at quarterback
—clear skin, flushed with life
      the wrinkles gone
         the thinning hair jet-black
    his eyes are glowing
       he has ripped through the pain
to the other side of it
    he turns his eyes to me
   and I start to speak
to apologize, but again I can't
      it is choked back inside me
he takes my hand
     in his iron grip
"Don't worry... I know..."

    he smiles, beatified through the pain
   his eyelids flutter
he is gone

    this time, he does not speak to me
        but I see behind his black eyes
  my own son, his grandson
      and a path of light opens
          running through the three of us

    his face goes under black
then deep violet, with gold specks
      and my body shakes—
        I lie there
    lighter, then lighter

      when my bones return
  I stand
    and these winged feet
        float me
    the rest of the way
          down the mountain

at trail head
    I come down on
five-man crew & their chief
    a brown woman
  filling out her shirt & jeans—
her prankster eyes
      match
    her green bandanna
(Ruth Roman on a better day)

    I jabber on
      through sun-cracked lips
    about sign up top
(no mention of the "weird" stuff)
      & somehow it comes out
    she is one-fourth Arapahoe

after we've smiled at each other
      & smiled again
    she sez "back to work"
      and leaves me there
          still grinning

the others nod and move ahead
        and I cruise down to Pebble Crik

        to find my quart of Oly
                pinned beneath some rocks
      press the chill brown glass
to my forehead—
        Thor's nectar
                through a glass darkly

      with shaky hand
              twist the silver cap
    and chug it down
Ah! Basho Buffo! Holy Holy Han Shan!
      the light
            cranks up three notches &
      I fall on my butt on the bank
          of this holy shoal
    and laugh
    and begin to cry
and laugh again

🀆

I call from Gardiner
      ask you to do up
             some homemade burritos
    your voice is kind
          but hesitant
  we hang up

    I could wash your feet
         I could sing of more sons
  and tell you how I feel
        but it's no use

as I walk to the truck
        the time has come:
I divide our love
      by truth
and come up wanting

    but it ends up in the soul
    and I must stand down
        to taste it anyway

Instructions

Trace the backbone to where it disappears.
There, gentians suck the color from the sky.
You will see dancers, barely visible,
stumbling through the aspen as if drunk.
When you hear a crow's call rise like hunger,
travelling south, turn and sit. A fine pollen
will settle on your hair and shoulders.
Bring no weapons. Several bears will cross you—
even if a grizzly raises up and paws the air,
hold your ground. Breathe. Speak sharply.

It will be years before you get here.
The first time, be alone. If you need me
look over your shoulder, fifty paces back.
Call and I will see with you through your eyes.
And on this morning, this first morning,
you will sense love, the skin laid out for you
to put on for the rest of your life. It
will be blue—not the color of mountains
as the sunlight fades or of mourning,
but the color of feathers and of eyes
and of old ones who live beneath the snow.

You will hear the rhythms of an ocean
and your body will rise in slow spirals
up to the high place. From there you will see
the deep obsidian face of your past.
Deny the terrors. Let the quick lightning
writhe through you to set root at the center
of the earth. It will turn your blood to vapor.
You will smell, then, something like gardenias,
but far beyond its wildest echoes, so
clean you will weep tears of tourmaline.

You will know when to come down. Follow the
old road, the glad ice on the stream of light.
There are no dams here. The bark on your hands
will be white, my son, your eyes green moons.
Begin running ahead of time, into time,
no matter—you can dream now, forever.

Notes

Daysweat
> The quotations on pages 25 and 26-27 are from poem 78 of Lao Tzu's ***Tao Te Ching***, translated by R.B.Blankney.

Ascent
> The King Boletus is *Boletus edulis*. My favorite Boletus, for its name and no other reason, is Miss Alice Eastwood's Boletus (*Boletus eastwoodiae*).
> The fly Amanita is *Amanita muscaria*.
> The destroying angel is *Amanita verna*.
> The coral mushroom is *Clavaria pyxidata*.
> The "cherry tomato lookalike" is the clasped twisted-stalk, *Steptopus amplexifolius*.

Over the Top
> The quotation on page 45 is taken from The Judgment of the Lu hexagram (The Wanderer), Book I, ***The I Ching***, translated by Wilhelm and Baynes.

Conflagration, September, 1988

for Dan and Bette Mongold

That very day my lungs give out,
I can't recall my own name.
I stay home from work.
I go to the class I teach
and end my sentences halfway through.
Maybe it's the central air
                we've just installed,
maybe it's Legionnaire's disease,
maybe. . .
after a week of this
I finally smell the smoke in the sky.
I breathe in
bits of atomized porcupine
of aspen limber pine and piss fir
of grizzly sow of coyote pups
of blue lupine and elk thistle—
My lungs understood
what my head had not.

Fourteen hundred miles away
my friends
lumber into Silvergate
with smoldering coats.

Back Country, Yellowstone

From behind the sun, blots of fire attach
to elk and ride them down the black ravines.
Their hooves drum meadows into bloom.
Blank in memory, blank in winter rain
the wild worship will boom down this music.
Here, there is no intelligence, no human
beard to sop the light away, no widow's
walk from which to wand the elk.

I look up from deadfall where I stand:
a brine hangs from the north face.
Above the rose escarpment, gilded blue,
a lifelong wind whose song weaves calumny,
and suddenly the wings grow dumb.
Here where the dead fall and fires speak
I hear a moist ear in the carcass of a larch.
A woman rain lisps a continent away.
Where does it exist? Underneath the mane
of the falls? Where human hooves have worshipped?
Where this slant wind honeycombs the bones?

Six chapters of our life are over,
dry horn left shattered by the targets.
If I could drain this bitter lie for you
and detonate your rage, you'd come to see
animals made visible in hissing light.
I would take you, pearl music, once again,
knee deep in Pebble Creek, and the rivers
of heaven would split inside this seed.

1989

Part II

Obsidian Point

Mt. Hornaday, northern Wyoming
August 1990

I

There is the face, pale, pocked, forbidding,
like Siamese twin monkeys, heads compressed
into their bodies. Crows fly from eyeholes.
In the foreground, an aspen grove comes at me
like a troupe of dancers edged in green.

At the foot of a massive Douglas fir,
small-horned, ruddy-barked and dead, there are
skullmaps, bone ciphers left by griz.
A legbone for a pipe, a lower jaw
for teeth, a crushed skull for medicine.
Last year I took the hooves for rattles.
The wince and stink of sodden hides
made the grasses crawl away from me.
The first time I'd been back since '75 —
just time enough to skirt the mountain's base.

Veer west, toward the crest of Hornaday;
deadfall piled like silvered pickup sticks.
Hoist up and run an angular course
which seems to have no end — maybe I can
get to Canada without touching ground.

A washout, deep as a crater left by a
thousand-pounder dropped from a B-52.
Quiet, but for virulent mosquitos.
A decent pond, lots of tracks in the mud.
Smart move to freeze my canteen overnight.

Then I see deep indentations where he
started down but didn't like the footing.

Perched halfway up an impoverished outcrop
I test the next handhold above me;
the stone appears to be cemented.
As I start to belly up the wall
like a legless thousand-pound lizardo
the stone pulls loose and hurtles into space.
I remember times when I'd hugged the rock,
paralyzed, for half an hour at a time.
I wedge up toward the top, growling,
knowing it's all the way or nothing.
And another outcrop, outcrop, outcrop.

There's an easy way up Hornaday —
follow the Rose Creek drainage
in from the other side. At its highest
Hornaday is only 10,036. But you'd
better have your head on straight.

Finally, open air and a 45° incline.
The air bites my lungs, throat catches, I cough.
No scent in the air — can't see or taste it,
but the smoke of fires west of here.

Platoons of flies mine gashes on my legs,
mosquitos drilling through my salty hide,
grasshoppers clacking brittle wings, like
ancient helicopters in formation.
I take out my peanut butter sandwich
and bolt it like a starving beagle.
Mid-day: the wax is melting on my wings.

When I finally reach the top, it's not, again.
All my bones jarred loose from their harnesses
but I force them upward, onward. At last!
I breach north of where I'd calculated,

north of the knoll where the benchmark is.
This skyline, these pale ruddy boulders,
my feet sinking in this brick dust gully —
we are exiles rushing back to reunion.

II

There in the distance, the sheep ponds.
A shape or two in the grass — can't make them out;
maybe they are scrub pines turned to bears
by my imagination, but trees rarely
solo up here. Snow droops the branches
and some take root, otherwise camprobbers
load up on seeds and cache them in the shade
where those forgotten sprout and form a colony.
Like the flowers, they survive in clusters.

Behind the bigger pond, a saddle
like the inward sweep of a woman's back,
down from curve of hip up to shoulder,
she, on her side, toward me. The pond,
a silver gash in the flat below.
Ticks of lavender, puffs of white, yellow
pinwheels in the braided beards of grass.
Beyond my destination, two ranges south,
the ridgeline is a faint blue wash.
The shapes by the ponds are larger than sheep —
maybe backs of boulders basking in the sun.
I am upwind, put a grove of limber pine
between the shapes and me. I can see them
through the branches — elk, not sheep. One cow
standing, neck bowed, and a sentinel off by herself.
Nothing visible but tan humps otherwise.
I step out from cover. The sentinel is up,
white rump, dark head and neckruff, then six
more heads, all ears in my direction.
A wave of movement — half the herd is up.
A central doe squares off against me, the other
half of the herd still supine. Heads of the
runners, like surging arrows. The does
put themselves between the upright danger
and their calves. One cow and a calf, the stragglers,

last to rise and bolt. At certain nodes
in the wave, a doe turns to face me, never
the same one. Five of the calves bunch up.
The spread is one-two-four-five-one and two.
They've turned tail, target rumps, listing
toward the leader, who has twenty yards on them.
They reach the base of the hill where one fork
of the trail rises over the saddle, the other
down a draw. They stop, one guard at each
flank, facing me broadside, the rest look back
over their shoulders. They string out again
down the draw, the sun silvering their backs.

Tough bouquets in the crumbly powder —
white aster, yellow mule's ear, purple phlox.
Not much hope if you aimed to grow things here —
collect the elkshit from the ponds and try to
build the soil, a twiggy fence to keep them out.
Or bait them in, through a course of boulders.

Their swelling numbers and the Fire of '88
have driven the elk to higher pasture.
This used to be such a quiet sheepy place,
but the elk's deep trails look permanent.

I slop through the first pond, with its
inlets, coves and branches, ankle deep,
in dry years almost nonexistent.

I skirt the big pond, heading for the rim.
What looked like a big turtleback is just
a hummock in the pond. Five squatty ducks
bob smugly in the riffles. A wet year —
pond twice the size that I remember it.

III

Walk through this country, and every time you
find this kind of vista, it's where they stopped —
someone's stash of worked pieces, chips and flakes.
Makes sense — if you were going to spend the day
chipping away at tools, do it where the air is clear,
the view goes round and your song will carry.

In this one spot, take inventory —
every hue and tone of chalcedony
all chipped from different epithermal veins.
The stones carry the names of ancient places:
sard from Sardis, chalcedony from Chalcedon,
agate from beside the Achates River, Sicily.

1. One side looks like undistinguished weathered bonechip. Tap it — it is much harder than bone. Turn it over and it's congealed gelatin or root beer candy, a few flecks of delicate pale coral, and this, surrounded by feta-white porcelain embedded with black obsidian islands. When you hold it to the sun, the root beer glows, perfect! You experience the liquidity of it, at the cataclysmic time of its formation.

2. Another three pieces of the same, more coral, more opaque.

3. All kinds of different materials melted at the same time in an agate, a fine etching, Dürer, on its surface.

4. Ocean-shell red, that you'd see in a big shell, white chips, violet-pink.

5. Chalky gray, shot through with warmer white, colors melded.

6. Opaque white, shattered and incorporated, melted into another medium.

7. A fine little scraper, the color of an ocarina — light jade striations, a pure glassy line runs through one end. Sea-green, blood in water. These colors only in this kingdom.

8. Red glinting veins sweep through to the warm light, flat against plane of the stone, deep, dense. A small bear's silhouette inside, heading east.

9. One green-black, another blue-black, another red-black, like Rothko's studies in black, subliminal. The red-black is the color you find on the innermost skeletal bones when you strip the meat off a roast chicken.

10. Blue-gray suspended in translucence, a shrill scalloped edge.

11. An old piece of oily junkyard rock which, from an aerial view shows two bright smoky bits of opal— "as above, so below"— replicating the two elk ponds on this meadow where I stand.

12. Beginning of a scraper, warm red.

13. A geode, diamond facets, permutations of glacial ice in the quartz. Bubbly interior. Turn it to the light, rivulets of red. Minute particles of soil spreading like microscopic vines through the surface of the crystal.

14. Obsidian point. Perfect. Harder, glinting plates, made under incredible heat. Dark smoke suspended in a glassy medium. Admiring something dangerous, like the blade of an Oriental knife. This to killabird killabird. You could chip this thin enough to hold it to the light and see your friends' changed faces.

15. Obsidian chips.

16. Two pieces, dark rich black with pale green bits in it, played off against a warm neutral coral. No painter but a genius would use these colors in combination. Almost like a dark European marble — one piece veined, the other speckled.

    There's a paradox built into all these materials — that they are so dense, yet so translucent.

    Even though most of these pieces are castoffs, the way the stone breaks leaves sharp edges, angular points.

17. Deep red — hue dark, tone dark — burgundy, but earthy tonality. Kept from being intense by cast of black.

18. Its cousin, more sheen, more polish.

19. A tiny geode, green verdigris surface, maybe stained by copper, maybe not — as if it had been hurled through jade. Pinkish insides.

20. Maybe a cast of a shell, a pointed helmet. Can see greenish light if you look inside its murky opening.

21. Another geode, miniature conglomerate on its surface. Another, its surface lightly mossed. Another, covered with land-locked barnacles.

22. Pure white quartz with honey-colored veins.

23. Another piece, which looks as if it has been fired.

24. Another, with black veins and a soreness running through.

25. Schist slabs, silvery reflections in their soiled surfaces.

26. Petrified wood, two pieces. One reddish, the other verdigris-green — maybe epidote, though.

27. Half a scraper. Blue-green veins, under the smooth surface of a princess's skin. And red arteries — both venous and arterial blood running through. Or a wall in Canyon de Chelly — same sense of hardness. Translucent. The rose muddies toward the base.

28. Spear point, obsidian, opaque, the end broken.

29. What was to be an ax head, rejected, purple-gray.

30. Several specula, like pointed heads of moles or voles.

31. Three chunks of petrified overcooked butterscotch pudding.

chert>sherd>shard

These Sheepeaters, seen by other tribes as
pushovers, and as beggars by the whites, must
have had an eye for beauty nonetheless,
or maybe this particular chappie had a flair —
neighbors traded bearclaw necklaces for the
lucent points and scrapers that he fashioned.

In the old days, I would have taken these —
this time, I put them back where they belong.

The peaks, in panorama: Baronette, Abiathar,
The Thunderer, Norris, Druid, Bison, Frederick,
and the distant ranges. What names did he
assign them as he chipped his way to twilight?

IV

I trudge up the bluff to find my spot —
more trees than I remember. Every open stretch
along the rim looks just like it, but not quite.
Finally I recognize the shape of the
nearby grove. The ground still smoothed bare,
the pale red boulder I rolled to mark it.
I sit down in the dust, the consistency
of rust on implements mixed with clay,
rained and snowed on for a million lifetimes.
Scrawl your name, read it in a hundred years.
I recall travois marks across the ground
along the Yellowstone, unwitting signatures.

In a heap of pale red conglomerate
a marmot, hidden but for his twitching tail.

Fifteen falls ago I'd climbed up here alone.
Brought a bag of cornmeal and a bunch of sage —
spread the sage and covered it with pine boughs.
Then sat, and waited. And chanted, and pushed,
and wept. No food with me, my only water
a handful, now and then, of crusted snow.
Three days, three nights inside the circle.

This place was my teacher, my Marpa;
the message in the rocks, the trees and plants,
the voice and posture of the birds and beasts,
the weather overhead, the moaning in the wind —
the teacher giveth, the teacher taketh away.

The sky is beetling, the rain sweeps in
from the northwest, thunder like the coupling
of 2,000 boxcars. Up here, in '75,
I'd heard explosions in the cloudless skies
and wondered if it were the thunder beings
calling me to take contrary paths.
An hour ago, though skies were overcast,
I heard the same dull boom due west and
realized it must be dynamite;
the veil of saintly pretense drops away.

My hiking crony in those days would always
abandon the heights with any cloud in sight.
The lore of lightning storms had gotten to him.
He always carried a Luger with him, too,
when we hiked in here. Last time, though,
packed his pistol but forgot his ammo clip.

The last time I was up here I could see
a chipmunk blink at a thousand yards.
I could move, at the crack of the bat, and make a
diving catch at full extension deep to left.
These days I play first base. Without glasses
I can still lash the ball by instinct,
but it's all a pointillistic blur.
And watch me drag that fridge around the bases.

From here, the pond casts no reflection —
blank lacuna in the sloped plateau
below me, window to the valleys south;
a piece missing from the puzzle landscape.

V

It had been a time of loss for me,
my father dead, my son and his mother gone.
Ah, Wilderness! But the only wilderness
was in my soul. I'd sat on this peninsula
of sorrow, knowing tomorrow might never come.

But the saved half of me bubbled up like a
mudpot full of shining stuff. For three days
visitors came to me — under the full moon,
halfway up the mountain, I was awakened
by a weight sprawled across my sleeping bag;
a black bear rummaging through my gear. No food,
so he shuffled up the hill, complaining.
Then, up top, when I'd become just another
hum in the landscape, chipmunks raced up and down
my arms as I sat in meditation, and
chickadees fluttered in the air above me
when I did a particular high-pitched chant.
The second night, after the moon had risen,
a twelve-foot rattler I'd summoned from some realm

beyond, shattered what I thought to be my body;
I returned to this world intact an hour later.
The next day, with the sun straight up, a flock of
gray and ochre butterflies descended on
the hillside down below. When they lifted off,
there were red droplets everywhere. And then a
bull elk came up from behind with lowered rack —
I forced myself to him through my eyes and he
pawed three times and cantered down the ridge.
Finally, I floated down the mountain. When I
rested in a cave behind a waterfall
my father's ghost came to me from the pines.

Two weeks later, when I left that life,
I didn't know that it would be for good.
I'd come down from my mountain stronghold
to front the world, or so it seemed.
It broke my heart to leave my son — my eyes
were fogged by tears for the two-day drive,
but to stay was suicide. I'd
forgotten just what buzzard days those were.

In those years after, my life had blossomed
then levelled off. Most of my dreams these days
are merely aberrations, or morning
conversations when we lie together.
Like some succulent in a desert place
or larva buried in the mud, I come
to life only under right conditions.

I list off all the women who've fallen
through my arms since then. Maybe my woundedness
attracted them, until they came to recognize
the scumbling rumdumb creature underneath
my youthful charm and sensitivity.

I'd wanted to have my family back,
to raise my son. Later, he made that choice;
his mother agreed to let him live with me.
I did a decent job — he is a man now,
in most ways a better one than I.
You were the one who made us that family
but I, as usual, wanted more than that —
more children, a better... everything.
My fantasies drained away our time,

rerunning old relationships, the door
ajar. And my need to cast the first stone.
In mirrors, I see the weight of betrayal,
wanting to tell you all of this, cut through
the knot, so you might finally trust me.
But not long distance, not by telephone.
Not today, not tomorrow, not next month.

Before I start down, I stand at the rim.
I shout your name and it follows itself
along trails below me, like young mountain sheep
returning to their place of rest.
Though it is sprinkling, I am parched.
I taste your name on my lips —
it satisfies me, the stick and whisper
of its single syllable of grace.

VI

Scooting down a hillside on my butt
I come out on a cliff between two pines;
the sunlight hits my face and stuns me.
And then a hummingbird, dusty green,
bathed in pollen, a giant green mote
in the sunlight, starts to dart by me
but hovers before my face, intent
on drilling through to my third eye.
I wave her away, a female broad-tail.
Then it comes to me: the bright red sweat-soaked
old bandanna wrapped around my noggin.

Coming down the denning side of the mountain.
Edge down crevices, slide down hillsides
on my butt, rip myself a dropflap in my shorts.
Halfway down. I stop for a blow and through the
trees across a deep gorge, 100 yards away,
is a big yellow grizzly, sitting on his duff
looking over to see what's causing such a ruckus.
Finally, he gets bored, falls to all fours and
shambles off. Missed my chance to strut and roar —
can't do much when you're standing at attention.

As I rumble onward, the hairs on my back
say he might appear from behind that giant

conglomerate egg down there in the spruces.

I must've cut a few degrees over
toward Druid Peak, and it's getting dark.
Don't want to be in here when it falls —
every snapped twig a black chimera.
The third time I've been up here alone,
first time with a map. The other times
instinct served me well, but now I'm lost.

Angle down a mossy gorge to a creek
which, by the map, will lead to Trout Lake
or Shrimp Lake or a gingerbread house.
Sink my face, my entire head in the
arctic ginger ale. So little waste
when I pee, it comes out colorless.
Wolf down the last of my soggy raisins.

It's levelling out. At twilight, a marsh.
I cut the edge but there is no edge. The shadow
and the whistle of a redtail pass above me.
I come out in a green pellucid meadow.
A Peaceable Kingdom kind of place,
I tell myself, then find the perfect skull
of a yearling mountain sheep, of a full
grown elk, of some kind of large rat, and
a scattering of bones from several carcasses —
my friend and mentor at his task of "harvesting."
I put the smaller bones in my knapsack
with the others and wrap the elk skull
in my poncho to carry under my arm.

The current's smooth around a horseshoe bend,
the bottom clear and sandy, the water
icy cold. I drench my face, suck long and deep.
Friends ecologically and politically correct
say watch out for *giardia*. But it *sounds*
benign, like a chubby New York politician.
I'm up and moving, I must be getting close.
Yes! Over a rise I recognize Trout Lake.
I unfold my map and see I'm at least a mile
from where I wanted. These feet are becoming
resentful of every step I take.
It is dark now. RVs whish along the highway
east to Cooke City. I wrap the pristine

elk skull tighter in my poncho and lift
my aching pistons toward the campground,
hoping a cop will stop and find my contra-
band mementoes. To get me off my feet.

VII

On the front seat of the car, there is
the note I wrote if I didn't make it back —
that tells you how much I care about you,
that tells my son to take the path of light,
that gives the numbers of three friends to call;
a little bit of cosmic melodrama.
I pop open the hatchback, change into
a fresh t-shirt. I reek of stale urine
and wino sweat. Chug some lukewarm 7-Up.
The sky has cleared to a cold indigo,
festooned with stars.

I say to myself, read those stars, my man.
Read the signs, they're everywhere around you.
Don't need a map for this, just pay attention.
Not the scrawny potholed roads abandoned,
not interstates, but the winding path
the heart takes when you give it all its head.

VIII

I may wake up here one morning, the
dew on my whiskers, not remembering
how I arrived. And was it a human
cry awakening me, a cry of flesh
touched into pieces? I have not been here
when the world is dead. Should I chance it?

Two paychecks away from straining Sterno
through a loaf of dumpster bread, or build
a vision like Van Gogh's which melts the wax
completely and it all spools by, the colors,
as you hurtle to the sea. And in a hundred years,
if there are one hundred left, the auctioneer
at Sotheby's will say "This original
manuscript *sold!* to the man in the
yellow hat, for 2.8 million dollars."
Or settle into that reflection
in your eyes, be that person, that lame buck
come to the back yard in winter, to eat
the cracked corn you've left out in a bucket,
to bear the heat of you at last.

Out of sight, out of mind, a kingdom not
of this world, but deep inside it. Faith,
faith, like teeth in an old jaw you find
or colored rocks left on a swerving cliff
it will remain, I will leave it for you.

Part III

A Season Of Poor Tents
(apologies to Gretel Ehrlich)

"Who shall ascend into the hill of the Lord? and who shall stand in his holy place?
"He that hath clean hands, and a pure heart; who hath not lifted up his soul to vanity, nor sworn deceitfully."
    Psalms 24:3-4

"As a dog returneth to his vomit, so a fool returneth to his folly."
    Proverbs 26:11

I boarded a 5 a.m. Greyhound in Iowa City, Iowa, my destination Sheridan, Wyoming, some 29 hours hence. When I entered the bus, I noticed an overwhelmingly acrid smell, as if the bus had recently been used as an exercise barn by the Budweiser Clydesdales. Immediately I recognized once again why I loathe traveling by bus and that I was in for the usual debilitating and demoralizing passage. It must be that I travel this way on occasion as a form of penance. Another possible reason is to make sure that my life isn't becoming too insulated.

In Omaha, during daylight hours, upon returning to the bus after our meal break, I saw a man spread a plastic sheet over his seat, including the surface of the headrest, then wrap himself in it methodically. Apparently, the Clydesdale smell was being generated by this man, by human sweat percolating underneath unbreathing plastic.

Farther into Nebraska, at another rest stop, I said to a fellow passenger sitting at a picnic table smoking, that sometimes I think I might prefer riding on top of the bus. He caught my inference and said that he had been putting up with the smell ever since Chicago. Just then the implied subject of our conversation wandered by with a can of Orange Crush he'd drug up from the depths of a huge many-layered hive of plastic bags he kept in the overhead luggage rack, this accumulation of plastic bags serving as his luggage. He walked in a kind of simpering drugged shuffle, talking to himself, giggling, rolling his head from side to side, in a deranged parody of a Hindu gentleman giving his assent. He took the can of Orange Crush over near the wall of the cafe and attempted to drink it in private, but he had trouble swallowing, sensing that some of us were watching him. He then rushed behind the cafe beyond our sight where we could hear him gagging. The other passengers just looked at each other and shook their heads.

When we reboarded, the man spread his plastic meticulously, then wrapped himself up in it again. It was clear that he was doing this partially for warmth, because the bus was a tad chilly, but primarily for hygiene. I'd noticed that he never purchased any prepared food at rest stops but dug deep into the recesses of his hive of plastic bags for packaged items, indicating to me that he was not about to trust food prepared by human hands. If you've ever worked in a sleazy diner or restaurant you doubtless have some idea of the substances which are often deposited in the mashed potatoes and gravy of unsuspecting customers, and could appreciate his suspicion. And, in this day of exotic communicable diseases, he did not seem comfortable leaning his face against the fabric of the headrest on which someone else may have drooled or sneezed or breathed infectious microbes; he was sealing himself in hermetically. I thought back to those days in my childhood and youth when I had accepted pillows from Pullman porters without the slightest concern for hygiene whatsoever.

After we reboarded in Grand Island and were on our way, a rambunctious curmudgeon wearing an Edinboro State sweatshirt and an umpire's cap, approached the cocooned man and sprayed air freshener all around the area where he was seated. Titters of amusement went up from some, belly laughs from others, but everyone agreed, in principle, with the impulse of the chap, despite the overtness of his gesture. The crew in the back seats was particularly taken.

The bus veered over to the shoulder and stopped. The driver, one Antonio Suttle, of Chicago, an affable bearish man, set his flashers, then rose and looked us over calmly. He began by chastising the young man, saying that his gesture was insulting, that he (Suttle) had already given us a spiel when he'd taken over back in Omaha about being tolerant of each other and that traveling long stretches in this manner is not natural and that you get what you pay for. He said these things in an even-tempered, controlled tone; he had the attention of everyone on the bus, including the jokers in the back.

At a later stop, Mr. Suttle took the odd man aside outside the bus, spoke with him for several minutes, then returned to the bus, where he pulled a clean tee-shirt from his own travel bag, a deodorant stick, some soap and a towel and gave them to the man. The man proceeded to the rest room of the nearby McDonald's from which he emerged several minutes later in the fresh tee-shirt. While the odd man had been away at these ablutions, Mr. Suttle had given us another talk about tolerance. Clearly, in his own mind he was just "doing his job." During the rest of the trip he had chatted up the folks in the front seats nonstop on a plethora of subjects revolving around television culture, such as the merits of "The Captain" on *Gilligan's Island*, versus "The Professor," until he was replaced by a new driver in Ogallala.

It is a week and a day later, the night of September 20th, 1991. I am at 8,800 feet, the temp is in the low 20's, snow is immanent. And I am wrapped up in a sheet of plastic. The situation is this: I am sleeping on the ground in a meadow on the side of Mt. Frederick, in Yellowstone Park, above the Lamar Ranger Station, in the Rose Creek drainage. During the last week of September 1975 I had come up here on important business and ever since then had wanted to return at precisely this time of year, to rekindle my fading images of this place and of those events. In '75 I had been prepared; this time, however, I had not brought any camping gear with me when I'd left Iowa, having opted instead to cart along the reference books I'd need to complete the writing projects I'd be working on. I figured that if the opportunity arose for me to come up here to Yellowstone, some six or seven hours from where I'd be based at the Ucross Foundation, east of Sheridan, that I could borrow camping gear. I asked around and was loaned a summer-weight slumber party L.L. Bean bag. I could have been more specific in my asking, but I'd let it ride, thinking I was over the first hurdle — being a beggar, I waived my choices. Now... what if it got *really* cold? They were, after all, predicting snow for these elevations. I had gone out to the new building they were working on at the foundation and bummed a roll of 3 mil plastic from the carpenters. I thought again of the man on the bus. Setting him aside, I knew that street people seem to survive wrapped up suchly, and after all, John Muir was known to head up into the Sierras for long stretches with just a stout coat to keep away the chill and a pocketful of raisins for sustenance. Taking his lead, I had purchased a six-pack of Shur-Fine seedless raisins at the Buttrey's in Sheridan — my only staples for the hike.

I had traveled up here to Yellowstone with Dale Newkirk, sculptor and fellow resident at Ucross. Dale had wanted to make the loop of Yellowstone and do some in-depth sightseeing. The plan had been that he'd drop me at the Lamar Ranger Station, where they were expecting me, I'd spend the night on Mt. Hornaday, then he'd pick me up at 6 p.m. the next day.

We didn't get to the Lamar Ranger Station until 5 p.m. and the ranger, Brian Chan, a sprightly man to whom I had talked on the phone earlier (to make special arrangements to stay overnight on Hornaday), said that he was reluctant to issue me the special back country permit to spend the night in an area with no designated campsites since it was already so late in the day. I assured him that despite my spare tire I was in excellent shape (a colossal stretch) and that I would push it until sundown. He said to me that they go out of their way to accommodate special requests like this but that they expect campers to go out of their way also. I told him that I understood this completely but that this was a rare opportunity for me and I'd come a good ways to undertake this pilgrimage. He said, with a crinkly smile, that he was still reluctant but that I seemed determined and he would consent. He signed the permit, gave me the requisite list of do's and don't's, then walked with me out past the corrals and pointed out to me how far I'd have to get before I stopped for the night. Seemed do-able to me, so I thanked him and set out.

After three hours of humping it without a break, up and up, I'd finally stopped in this very meadow just as the sun was plummeting. Though the temperature had been in the high 30's or low 40's when I'd left the ranger station, I was dressed in tee-shirt and nylon shorts, bandanna coiled around my head. Ranger Chan had commented that he heats up pretty fast, too, and that he'd probably dress the same way. And in fact my tee-shirt was already sopping with sweat. I rolled out the plastic, rolled out the Bean bag, hauled off the nylon shorts, put on jeans and denim shirt, sweatshirt with hood, and down vest. There would be no time to change to a dry pair of socks; I was already wracked by shivers and realized that I'd have to dry my tee-shirt, socks, etc. with my own body heat and that my soggy shoulder-length hair might become a liability — maybe it would freeze into a helmet of ice before the night was over. I put my penlight in one pocket of the down vest, my Gerber folding knife in the other; I'd need to see what I was stabbing. I slipped into the sleeping bag and cranked up my thermostat. I thought of that Tibetan sect which has its initiates sit naked next to a hole in the ice and then wrap themselves in sheets which have been dipped in the freezing water. Their task is to dry sheet after sheet with nothing but their own body heat.

Before the light had vanished completely I had spotted two elk at the head of the meadow and as it grew dark, nearby bulls began their extraterrestrial bugling — it was that time of year. While inside my sorry excuse for a sleeping bag, I wormed over to one edge of the plastic, grasped the edge and rolled myself up in it, with about two feet overlapping both my head and feet. As my breath condensed on the plastic it formed a rime of frost, and with each breath, since my face was only a short distance from it, the now-rigid plastic would squeak and sigh, a malignant apparition, no doubt, to nocturnal passersby.

The wind was coming up and it smelled like snow. My lungs were tightening. I'd brought along my Ventolin inhalator for my asthma and it appeared that I'd be needing it soon. I unrolled myself, got out the penlight and went over to my Bean shoulder bag, which was hanging in a piss fir. It was just looped over a limb about six feet up — if Buster Bear wanted my raisins he could have 'em. My stuff was supposed to be ten feet up and four feet out, but it was too cold to abide strictly by regulations. I took two hits of the Ventolin and was shivering mightily. When I got back in the bag I had one of those spells in which you shake so violently that it feels as if your teeth will shatter into bits. I slipped the edge of the Bean bag over my mouth and breathed through the musty material. Would this intensify my asthma and cause my alveoli to shut down completely? The thought crossed my mind that I might have to make my way out of here in pitch or semi-pitch darkness down through deadfall and sinkholes and who-knows-what-else. I'd done this kind of thing once, on a hiking companion's insistence, and it had turned out to be almost suicidal. On that occasion I'd finally set my heels and refused to proceed. If what I was really after was some kind of ordeal, if I was in search of austerities, such a venture would certainly qualify. I curled up in a fetal position, hugging myself tightly, and could tell that my body temperature was evening out, for the time being, anyway. I noticed also that the sleeping bag was getting wet from where I was breathing through it. Was I so well-insulated by the plastic that this would happen all over the surface of the bag? Would the surface of the bag eventually freeze? Would this form a layer of insulation? Or would I become a human ice cube? The moon was two days from being full. The clouds were whipping across it, and they looked and smelled like snowclouds. It's not as if I did this sort of thing very often and what did I know about snowclouds anyway? What did I know about anything? After all, I'd had a desk job in Iowa for the past ten years, in a windowless office, and my life had hardly been tied to the rhythms of the outdoors. In the past, though, my instincts had worked pretty well for me in such circumstances. Had that been dumb luck? What in the hell was a 48-year-old overweight townie doing up here this time of year in a summerweight sleeping bag wrapped in a sheet of plastic?

An elk bugled just below me. And it sounded as if something was rummaging nearby, but my flashlight had a range of five feet and when I put that ridiculous fiber optic attachment on it that made it look like a field surgeon's proctoscope it worked even less efficiently. What's more, the sounds of the plastic squeaking and whining masked almost everything else but the elk music and the roaring wind. It would have been pacific to watch the stars wheeling in the heavens but it was too cloudy to see much more than the obvious constellations anyway; I kept drifting in and out of sleep. I was damn tired, but the paranoid part of me, that part including the warning alarm in my lungs, was not about to let me sink too far below consciousness. Once, many years ago, a friend and I had snowshoed up past Cooke City and had gotten caught in a blizzard. We dug into a snowbank for the night to let the blizzard pass, but I was awakened in a panic several hours later to discover that the wind has sealed over our entrance — the alarm had worked. Thinking of that time eighteen years ago, I drifted into shallow dreamless sleep.

Some time during the night, there was a jerk on the tight wiring in my lungs which ran up through the bridge of my nose — I came into blurred consciousness. Behind my shallow wheezing I heard a sound I couldn't quite make out. Maybe it was the crunch of feet, or hooves or paws in the dry red-brown pine needles under the nearby trees. Then another sound, vaguely familiar. I squirmed my head out of my stiff plastic cocoon. It was the girlish titter of the man on the bus. He was standing under the trees; hence, it was too dark to see his face. I saw him only in silhouette, his hip canted to one side in a kind of exaggerated contrapposto. He was dressed in tee-shirt and trousers, but did not appear to be bothered by the cold. I could see his breath. I noted that the only thing I could smell was pine needles. He noted this also and tittered at me again. There was something better-than-thou about the titter. Wrapped in plastic, eh? I didn't speak. He wasn't going to speak. What his presence said was "I am here, and I'm making you squirm like a worm. Is it my *color?*... or my sexual... *pref*erence? Or both? Let's get down to it, my man." I'd spent much of my life going out of my way to commit acts of color-blindness. Had I been fooling myself all along? When I wrote about this later, as I invariably would, would I not mention the man's color, so that the reader would grok that I am an upright politically-correct white liberal? I, who despise political correctness. Did it mean that my fascination and innate scorn for him had something to do with my being attracted to him? Or that there were leanings buried under my own macho hetero behavior? I'd always paid lip service to the idea that you mock in others what most troubles you about yourself. Why had Antonio Suttle been the only one who had enough decency to come to his defense, while I myself had been content to smirk along with the communal joke? Was this the result of my being raised in the Fifties and having attended an all-male prep school? Of privilege, of being a card-carrying member of the dominant society? Or, having been raised a Baptist, was I presuming myself guilty until proven innocent? *Gee HAWW!* Give it up! Drop it! Cut yourself loose, man! All this babble in the course of a nanosecond. He tittered again, softly, and shifted the weight to his other leg, and then faded.

　　　　　　　　　　🐾

　　When I awoke I could see the cold blue of the predawn sky through the plastic, which was entirely frosted over. But there was no dusting of snow on the plastic and I had no subliminal memory of snow ticking on its taut surface; I had made it through the night, and snow would not be a factor in the remainder of my pilgrimage. A good time to attempt some usually fruitless horizontal meditation. I kept drowsing off until about 7 o'clock when I squirmed out of the tunnel of stiffened plastic and frozen sleeping bag. I tapped and scratched off as much of the ice on the lip of the sleeping bag as I could, rolled it out flat and did the same to the plastic. I would leave it there to catch some rays while I skirted the perimeter of the meadow to see what I could see.
　　The first thing I noticed abut ten yards from me was a big pile of fresh bearshit. He'd been eating pinenuts, probably, judging from the granulated and regular consistency of the scat.

I didn't have the interest to pick through to see if there were undigested remnants of other kinds of food. Maybe there would be some rosehips. Clear why the creek is called Rose Creek; on the way up, there were rosehips everywhere. Just the right time of year to eat them, too — after the first frost has firmed them up. Must be beautiful when they are in bloom; worth a trip up through the same drainage during that time of year.

The only stressful part of my climb the day before had been when I'd encountered some cliffs. When I'd gone at Hornaday from the Pebble Creek side I'd always run into several stages of cliffs and crumbly rock in general. I had come in this way, a more gradual climb, to give myself a break for once. The distance was greater but according to the map there were few cliffs. Thus far that had been the case. Anyway, even the cliffs had been covered with rosehips. So, for a break, halfway through my crisscrossing of the ledges, I'd taken my dinner break (one minibox of raisins and a slug from my water bottle) and picked a big pocketful of rosehips. I'd transferred them to the breast pocket of my denim shirt in my bag. They would be my mid-morning snack the following day when I reached the top of Hornaday. I'd frozen my water bottle the night before — a great idea for early August, but not for late September.

I skirted the edge of the meadow, particularly the rock-cluttered apron just before the meadow falls off at a 45⁰ incline through the timber; this is where, with an excellent view of the Lamar Valley, I expected to find some pieces of chalcedony which had been worked. I found lots of interesting rocks, but nary a chip left from human activity. I followed the apron as it swung east toward Mt. Frederick, then, when it petered out, did a left-face back toward my gear, where I was confronted by the petrified stump of a Douglas fir (I presumed) with a bonsai garden growing on top. I snapped off a couple of shots of it with my old reliable Minolta, 50 mm. lens, then replaced that with the 135 for landscape panoramas of the surrounding ranges as I wound my way up to Hornaday.

Back at my campsite I rolled up the sodden sleeping bag and the by-then-thawed plastic. Even though there was a real bite in the air, I changed out of my denim overlayer and slipped on my nylon shorts so that I was dressed just as I had been yesterday. I rolled my bandanna and tied it in place around my forehead, pushed my prescription sunglasses up on the bridge of my nose and pointed my arthritic dogs uphill.

As I strode along, three pieces of Jim Harrison's "Passacaglia on Getting Lost" came back to me, like belches after a satisfying meal — "the well-equipped Republican clones you see marching like Hitler youth up and down the spine of the Rockies" — then "on the tops of mountains I've seen their cocaine wrappers and fluorescent shoestrings. At five thousand feet in the Smokies there were tiny red piss-ants crowded around a discarded Dalkon shield" — and finally "A trail, other than a game trail, is an insult to the perceptions." Well, no Dalkon shields, no Republicans, no man-made trails — yet. And I figured it would stay that way up there for quite a few years, unless the progeny of James Watts reared their reptilian pates. I recalled that, somewhere in the *Tao Te Ching* there are a couple of lines which say something like "the trail won't lead you anywhere of consequence, so get off it and bushwhack if you expect to make the grade." This country is meant to be walked in plain brown wrapper, not day-glo teal and fuchsia high tech gear. What will their excuses be when they come before John Muir at the Redwood Gates of Heaven?

    I spotted the bear just as I was about to head up the ridge — he was a black, not that big, but bigger than I by far, lounging on his side, playing casually with something on the ground in front of him, rolling the side of his face on whatever it was, like a cat with catnip, slowly and musingly. I edged toward him in a halting graduation step and snapped off a few shots with the Minolta, the 135 lens in place. For some reason, though there was no wind to speak of or through, he didn't hear the clicks. And what there was was a crosswind, anyway, so he didn't scent me. Finally he did pick up my presence, scanned, spotted me, righted himself and lumbered up the hill double-time with his ears laid back. Part of me was pressing the issue so that I might get a shot fit for an *Argosy* cover circa 1950, as he charged me with fangs exposed. But the rest of me knew that the bear and I were on the same tether. Most likely it had been his scat near my sleeping bag, deposited the previous night as I slept in my wheezing plastic cocoon. A descendent, no doubt, of the rube who rousted me from my sleeping bag that night 16 years ago under the full moon. My med'cin — Honeypaws, Chinnychin, come out to greet me, ag'in. But this b'ar was young enough to be my son, even in bear years.

    I came up on the spot where he'd been sprawled and found no trace of what he'd been rolling his face on; I even got down on my hands and knees and sniffed the spot thoroughly — nada.

    Up across the saddle from Frederick to the backside of Hornaday. Some view! Clicked off a few shots for the panorama I'd piece together later. Took another few steps, and did it again. Some day I'd go from there to Cutoff Peak — to the north, and beyond. If I'd had a little tripod those pans would have fit together perfectly.

   I was on the hindend of the main plateau overlooking the sheep ponds on Hornaday. I'd never seen the terrain coming at it from this direction. When I'd been up here before, those many years ago, my head had been in another place, anyway. Hornaday was so exotic to me, and had been so central to my entire imagination since then, that I thought of it as home. I locked down on it with my inner eye looking for traces, clues. I came up on the rim of the plateau, dropped my gear and finished the last of my melted water. What was left was still frozen, rattling around in the plastic bottle. But there were patches of crusty snow I could scratch a handful of, stuff into my mouth, or rub across my forehead. Ah!

   I clicked off the last three shots — nothing left for the trip back down. *Thank God!* No reason to document it anywhere but in my head. With *my* head, though, there was reason to doubt the data. I checked my miniature alarm clock — 12:15, it said. Didn't want to miss my 6 p.m. rendezvous with Dale. The sun felt good on my legs.

   The grass below in the meadow was yellow, a pale yellow. Sixteen years ago it had been yellow, too, but in my mind I remembered it as being quite green. Couldn't have been, no matter how mild a year. I could remember the details clearly, as if I were looking at it right then, but the grass had not been yellow. Hell, maybe it had been purple! The weather *had* been milder then — the entire time I'd been up there and the whole week before we'd had a beautiful Indian summer. I couldn't have invented finer weather. To most, I suspect, this would be a bleak place, little to recommend it but the view. No blue ribbon trout stream, alpine lake or waterfall. But this was where I took place, or at least had taken place once for three days back when. A mean environment, fit for an anchorite, but too high for the scorpion and the viper. The trick now was to get my soul tumescent once again. I'd romanticized that this was probably going to be my last time up here, but this "ascent" had been so easy that I knew I'd be back again.

   I remembered wondering, back in '75, if maybe the Thunder Beings had been talking to me, calling me, when I was up there. But I hadn't paid it much mind because the call was not strong and I wasn't about to become a contrary, having to do everything backwards for the rest of my life. Seemed that for most of my life I'd either done things the hard way or just plain bass-ackwards. Either that or taken the slouch's route — never the middle path. But I'd discovered, when I had been up there in '90, that it was dynamiters off in the distance somewhere — the same sound at the same distance, and not thunder.

   I took out a handful of rosehips and, with my front teeth, worried the leathery scarlet skin from around the ball of seeds. After about the fifth one, I figured the seeds must be good roughage, too. Then I chomped down the last box of raisins — my lunch. I knew this combination would bring on indigestion for the remainder of the afternoon but maybe I'd burn it off. When I had been up here two summers ago I'd thought I would find my "power spot" from the '75 visit, but the angle out over the valley to the south hadn't seemed right from any place where I'd stood. I traipsed up and down the ridge looking for that frame in my memory. I finally settled on a place which was closest to what I'd remembered, but knew, deep down, that the spot was wrong. I'd marked it anyway, with a small boulder. I decided to reconnoiter again this time. I came to a place which looked more familiar, slightly, than any of the others, though it seemed much farther up the line. And then I'd looked down and spotted a three-inch long piece of skinny braided nylon cord, old and weathered, almost invisible. It had been left from my stay up there in '75 — an inadvertent tag end of the rope with which I'd tied my sleeping bag to my pack frame. I don't like to leave traces or markers or blazes but this one was a nice affirmation, that I had been, in actuality, there. That it had not been some imaginary expedition. It had been the moment in which my inner life had reached its highest pitch ever. And the more I thought back on it, the more unreal it became, like a figment of my dream life. I took off my shirt and toodled down toward the saddle which led to the open course below.

   Near the cluster of piss fir guarding the southern entrance to this knoll I squatted to defecate — leaving a small cowflop, loose and greenish — my burger, fries and chocolate shake from the fast-food place in Cody the previous afternoon. I used some dry grass to wipe myself, scraped a hole, and covered the entire mess with some rocks. After all, Harrison might be along any minute and recognize my spoor.

   It has been my experience that after a few days on the trail the body straightens out, and produces nice little deer turds with no need for wiping. Or, if you're really cooking on all burners, no solid waste at all. When I'd been up here the summer before, in the heat of August, my body had been sloughing off months of self-abuse. I had been aware of myself going through the changes, layer by layer, odor by odor. After a week up here in the heat, steadily on the move, maybe I'd smell right, like Saint

Theresa, not some bluecoat fed on beans, coffee, venison and grog.

So I sat down on this spot where, sixteen years ago I had opened myself. This felt, to me, like it must feel for a W.W.II veteran on returning to a place like Mt. Suribachi. Let me modify that — I am not a warrior — I've never claimed to be any kind of warrior. To do battle with an armed human enemy takes a much braver person than I who had come up here back then and battled self-created demons and welcomed cosmic visitors. They were no less real to me, however, and no less formidable, than if they had been Japanese soldiers. But not a parallel situation. The point of being a warrior, anyway, is to defend those who cannot defend themselves. I could defend myself, could walk away at any time. I had gone through several harrowing moments up here during those three days in late September of 1975 but I had wanted it to happen, had even sought it out, and there had been no time for fear anyway. And back then I always seemed to know how far I could push myself. I do not believe in the idea of a "spiritual warrior" — to me, this is a New Age invention which trivializes genuine warriorhood. Would that warriorhood, though, was never a necessity, anywhere in this world. 1975. I remembered that having more kids had been much on my mind. It seemed unlikely at that point — maybe, I thought, I should put my energy, such as it was, into helping those kids who already existed, rather than creating more of them. I was pushing 50, my hair was thinning in the back; a nice monastic bare spot seemed on its way. And my girth had increased — I was starting to look like a stand-in for Marlon Brando. Before I had shaved, the year before, several people had said I reminded them of Orson Welles. Aside from that, I had not a single peso in savings, my salary had flatlined, and I had no visions of big projects on the horizon. Other than the rest of my life. Which was rapidly creeping up on me. I recalled *Proverbs* 21:16 —"The man that wandereth out of the way of understanding shall remain in the congregation of the dead." Really! Snap out of it, chap!

Down below in the flat there were no creatures at home and it didn't appear there would be. No fourleggeds, anyway; but a butterfly wafted by – small, black-winged with red markings. Maybe it had been a flock of these which had descended on me back in '75 and not the lighter ones I remembered when I'd finally gotten around to writing about them years later. I found a dead specimen of the same species on the ground and pressed it in my small notebook. I scouted the rim of the plateau double-time to get in as much of it as I could — oh, to have it such that I could sit in one spot for even three days again and leave my small self and take root.

I cruised with snout to the ground, looking for telltale chips and points — find them, examine them, put them back. Given the shiftiness of this soil, I tried to imagine from whence these elusive pieces had been washed, over the last hundred years and more since anyone had sat and chipped at them. I found a few, looked them over, then it was time to go. I hoofed it back up the ridge, picked a few sprigs of pale already freeze-dried flowers, pressed them in my notebook, then cinched up my gear. I turned to face south one last time, to look across the sweep of the distant ranges. Home, again. "Thanks. May I walk in beauty. I will be back to visit you again, maybe next time with a companion." I turned and began my return.

※

The trip up via Rose Creek had been incredibly easy — only a heyoka or an idiot or a maddog homeboy Englishman out in the noonday sun would have come up through the rocks on the south or east faces of Hornaday — the way I had ascended all the other times. Going back this easy way, I would get to the ranger station with time to spare. Just run the ridges, keeping to the high ground.

I was doing pretty well until I angled down toward what I assumed was the appropriate drainage, but there was more and more of it, and none of it looked familiar, and I was getting drier and drier. Lots of elk sloshing through the myriad criks, none resembling Rose Creek. I knelt and sucked in some of the barely-moving water — *giardia* be damned! It was evident that plenty of elk had watered, pissed and defecated there, but I would take the risk with the respite.

Finally the ground was starting to level out and there were more and more aspen. Ahead was what appeared to be a wee bit of soggy ground which I should slog across to save time. On the other side of this fen was a bull buff'ler in repose which my imagination had concocted from a fallen Doug fir stump twisted in just the right conformation. As I approached, the buff'ler stump remained stock still. I could avoid crossing this muck, but it would be wider down below, so I decided to just skim across it there. With my first step, I was in up to my chest. I let my other leg settle into the sucking sulfurous goo and craned my neck to see if there was anything I could grab ahold of. I pitched my now-encrusted knapsack and Bean bag onto the bank behind me — thank God my arms were free. As I started to maneuver my feet, the Doug fir stump rose from its knees and moved toward the edge of the bog, to see what I, the intruder, would do. Obviously he'd witnessed this predicament before. He was a big hummer. And I was at the edge of his territory. I didn't have any idea of how to gauge a bull's age, but it seemed that this guy was a retiree. Clearly, though, he couldn't get at me. He stood there staring at me with his shiny little eyes. I spoke to him: "Grandfather, I mean no harm to you, just passing through... on my way out to the asphalt path below, down where the guys in khaki grow." Then I turned myself around. Slowly. With great effort. My lightweight boots were laced on tightly, otherwise I'd have lost one or both in the quagmire.

Fortunately, right behind me was a knobbly fallen cedar, next to where I'd stepped off the trail into this mess. Not rotten yet — possibly decent leverage. I could see it now — if I didn't pull myself out of this: eventually they'd come out looking and there I would be with just my head sticking up out of the slime with the stupid inept penlight clenched between my teeth. Or maybe they wouldn't find me — at least the mud would be good insulation for the night. If I sank in *all* the way, my knapsack and Bean shoulder bag would be good clues for where to look unless some critters decided to take off with them. I envisioned some wily coyote watching from a distance, amused at this greenhorn's dilemma. If I did succumb, I'd be well preserved, like those guys they had exhumed from the peat bogs in England. And my pin-headed flashlight was the antithesis of the flashlights in the old *Boy's Life* Eveready ads — its beam would *never* lead them to me. Also, I'd be close enough to the shoulder bag to unravel the plastic again to make a tent — but this time I wouldn't have to worry about my nether parts sticking out in the cold — I'd just need to keep a cool head.

So I completed my turn in the quagmire. I determined that I could get just enough purchase on the fallen cedar to haul myself out of the muck. If this had been the year before, maybe not, with a compression fracture in my left forearm on the mend. The buffalo was real interested in what I was doing. With the primordial ooze sucking away at my boots at the force of several G's, I emerged slowly, carefully; the Man-Called-Horse's-Tookus. The buffalo still there but starting to get bored — his eyes glazing over.

As I sat and caught my breath on the mossy path, I thanked the Great Mystery for allowing me yet another escape, and for this lesson in paying closer attention to details, to reading the text in front of me. I scraped off what muck I could, using a stick I snapped off the fallen cedar, thanked the cedar profusely, patted it, wished it a pleasant decomposition, etc. Then I slung on my gear and got moving — I had not counted on *this* particular delay.

I headed downhill to where the marsh oozed over a bank toward yet another tributary of Rose Creek, while adopting a subservient forelock-touching posture toward the bull — his interest in me having revived. So now I was on solid ground, stinking, and soaked through. Oh, that this too, too sullied flesh would be transported by a flight of sultry brunette angels out of this place! The bull had an open downhill shot at me from up there but his expression was more quizzical than confrontational. That was his expression, but his size said otherwise. I'd never witnessed firsthand the charge of a bull buffalo but it was obvious to me that he'd be on me, if he wanted to be, before I could reach the shelter of the nearby trees. I continued my Groucho walk on a diagonal away from him. Soon I was through the trees, out of the woods, as it were, and I didn't look back. The ranger station must be just over the next hill — I was running out of time. As I sidehilled along the foothills the knotty roots of the sage and the rocky soil begin to take their toll on my cramped, abraded and now sloshy feet, each step becoming a station of my via dolorosa. Finally, I came over a rise and spotted the station down there below me — still some distance. I dipped down to what, finally, was Rose Creek and passed through a skull and antler display on the stumps and branches of trees. I assumed that this was where the rangers had stashed the relics they found in the environs, since no one is supposed to take them from The Park. I was not about to test my luck by choosing one for my collection and hiding it in my gear.

🐾

I am inside my sleeping bag, such as it is, next to the pay phone at the Lamar Junction. The sun has gone down. The gas station is closed, the lodge is closed, the rest rooms nearby are locked. I arrived at this situation in the following way — when I returned to the ranger station, the other ranger, Colette (a great gal, a perfect gal, for this kind of country, this kind of life or any kind of life), told me that Dale had called and that he'd be delayed, for several hours — his truck had broken down and he'd spent the day at the Old Faithful service station waiting for a part to come in, a water pump, to be exact. When it wasn't clear initially whether the part would actually get there in time for the mechanic to fix Dale's rig I began to let my mind ramble in its predictable squirrelly fashion: I could hitch a ride up to Gardiner with Colette who was going to a dance with her husband (unfortunately) and call any number of friends in Bozeman and have a night of it. Fantasy trysts with old girlfriends paraded seductively through my head. At that moment I felt like St. Anthony in that Schoengauer etching, with all those spooks and bugaboos pestering him. We have seen the enemy and he is within. Then Dale had called and said that he'd meet me at Lamar Junction at about 8:30. Colette was heading out to the dance at about 6 and said she'd drop me off. A great no-nonsense gal, wily, not easy to flatter.

Anyway, so here I sit, in my stinking clothes, still soaked through, no chance to dry off, no change of clothes, wrapped in my sleeping bag huddled next to the only light, that of the pay phone. I must look suspicious, like an escaped mental patient, or someone coming down from a bad trip, because not one of the several persons who've stopped to use the phone even acknowledged my presence, asked me if I was waiting for a ride or needed help. I have eavesdropped on some fairly boring conversations, but I did learn that Slough Creek is *the* spot to catch cutthroat trout. I called home, making the situation sound a trifle worse than it actually was. It was true nonetheless that I was sitting in this summerweight bag in sopping clothes with the temperature down to about 20 degrees again. When I had talked on the phone my teeth had chattered. But I *had* hammed it up: the night in the plastic sheet and the plunge in the buffalo wallow and the face off with the old feller made for an impressive tale. And it's nice to be loved, even long distance, even over the phone. It's nice.

The man on the bus: I imagine, to some of the people who have stopped to use the phone, that I am that same man. But, again, I am here by choice — I chose to spend the night up there wrapped in a sheet of plastic. Where was the man on the bus going? Who was waiting for him? Had he any choice? I can't answer those questions, and part of me is afraid to know the answers. Am I really much different from Harrison's Republicans, after all?

This little jaunt up Hornaday and back, including its pitfalls, has been good for me, reassuring, more than anything else. That I will be back, that I am not at the final portals. But without someone there at home I doubt that I would feel this way. I doubt because I am a doubter by nature though I do not like doubting. I hate it, in fact. And, without that someone, I would hate myself instead of just resenting or despising myself, which is my usual state. "Delight is not seemly for a fool." — *Proverbs*

19:10. I am separate, always in more than one place at a given time.

On Mt. Hornaday I had been whole. At least once, I had felt what it was like. At least once I had been to the mountain. At least once. I have always been running away from something. And tonight I can feel it in my blood that I will be able get there again, that I can run *to* something for a change, maybe even slow down to a confident saunter by then, and that maybe, just maybe, I can meet myself up there another time. Then I will be ready for the final leg of this race.

Coda

1

   to flower and ripen
  by inexorable black water
   a meticulous pool
that pours down the shoulders
     as regular as mercy
  and black sand
spilling from the treetops

  a deer comes
    shiver and leap
blue calls
  talk with bear tracks
riding the updraft
  on the long
    curve of invisibility

2

the light circles once more
  turning and rolling
in the windless air
  the nameless morning
infectious
they must have been here
    tattered in underbrush
I must change my direction
I have changed my direction
    my direction is set
  I must change it

3

      the seed
  catches
           in the humus
            of the wind's
     chords
        a song
             that flits
    across your face
               a passage
            frayed to its limits

            somewhere
                     along the silent
  silence
          buds open
       black as any darkness
  you find
        familiars
  who let you
    know the light of fate
      the fate of light
      when you can say
it is finished

Author

Ken McCullough's most recent books are *Travelling Light* (1987), and *Sycamore • Oriole* (1991). He has received numerous awards for his poetry including the Academy of American Poets Award, a National Endowment for the Arts Fellowship, a Pablo Neruda Award, a Galway Kinnell Poetry Prize, the Capricorn Book Award, and the New Millennium Poetry Prize. His poetry has appeared in a wide variety of magazines and journals. He has received grants from the Witter Bynner Foundation for Poetry, the Iowa Arts Council, and the Jerome Foundation to continue translating the work of Cambodian poet U Sam Oeur, survivor of the Pol Pot regime. Coffee House Press published *Sacred Vows*, a bilingual collection of U Sam Oeur's work in 1998 and McCullough and U are working on U's autobiography, *Crossing Three Wildernesses*, which will be published by Coffee House. McCullough lives in Winona, Minnesota. He was adopted into the Minconjou band of the Lakota Nation in 1993.

1975   **1991**